PENGUIN CLASSICS

THE SICKNESS UNTO DEATH

SØREN AABYE KIERKEGAARD was born in Copenhagen in 1813, the youngest of seven children. His mother, his sisters and two of his brothers all died before he reached his twenty-first birthday. Kierkegaard's childhood was an isolated and unhappy one, clouded by the religious fervour of his father. He was educated at the School of Civic Virtue and went on to enter the university, where he read theology but also studied the liberal arts and science. In all, he spent seven years as a student, gaining a reputation both for his academic brilliance and for his extravagant social life. Towards the end of his university career he started to criticize the Christianity upheld by his father and to look for a new set of values. In 1841 he broke off his engagement to Regine Olsen and devoted himself to his writing. During the next ten years he produced a flood of discourses and no fewer than twelve major philosophical essays, many of them written under *noms de plume*. Notable are *Either/Or* (1843), *Repetition* (1843), *Fear and Trembling* (1843), *Philosophical Fragments* (1844), *The Concept of Anxiety* (1844), *Stages on Life's Way* (1845), *Concluding Unscientific Postscript* (1846) and *The Sickness unto Death* (1849). By the end of his life Kierkegaard had become an object of public ridicule and scorn, partly because of a sustained feud that he had provoked in 1846 with the satirical Danish weekly the *Corsair*, partly because of his repeated attacks on the Danish State Church. Few mourned his death in November 1855, but during the early twentieth century his work enjoyed increasing acclaim and he has done much to inspire both modern Protestant theology and existentialism. Today Kierkegaard is attracting increasing attention from philosophers and writers 'inside' and outside the postmodern tradition.

ALASTAIR HANNAY was born to Scottish parents in Plymouth, Devon, in 1932 and educated at the Edinburgh Academy, the University of Edinburgh and University College London. In 1961 he became a resident of Norway, where he is now Emeritus Professor of Philosophy at the University of Oslo. A Fellow of the Royal

Society of Edinburgh, he has been a frequent visiting professor at the University of California, at San Diego and at Berkeley. Alastair Hannay has also translated Kierkegaard's *Fear and Trembling*, *Either/Or*, *Papers and Journals* and *A Literary Review* for Penguin Classics. His other publications include *Mental Images – A Defence*, *Kierkegaard* (*Arguments of the Philosophers*), *Human Consciousness* and *Kierkegaard: A Biography*, as well as articles on diverse themes in philosophical collections and journals.

KIERKEGAARD

The Sickness Unto Death

*A Christian Psychological Exposition
for Edification and Awakening by*
ANTI-CLIMACUS

Edited by
S. KIERKEGAARD
Translated with an Introduction and Notes by
ALASTAIR HANNAY

PENGUIN BOOKS

PENGUIN BOOKS

Published by the Penguin Group
Penguin Books Ltd, 80 Strand, London WC2R 0RL, England
Penguin Group (USA), Inc., 375 Hudson Street, New York, New York 10014, USA
Penguin Books Australia Ltd, 250 Camberwell Road, Camberwell, Victoria 3124, Australia
Penguin Books Canada Ltd, 10 Alcorn Avenue, Toronto, Ontario, Canada M4V 3B2
Penguin Books India (P) Ltd, 11 Community Centre, Panchsheel Park, New Delhi – 110 017, India
Penguin Books (NZ) Ltd, Cnr Rosedale and Airborne Roads, Albany, Auckland, New Zealand
Penguin Books (South Africa) (Pty) Ltd, 24 Sturdee Avenue, Rosebank 2196, South Africa

Penguin Books Ltd, Registered Offices: 80 Strand, London WC2R 0RL, England

www.penguin.com

First edition published in Danish as *Sygdommen til Doden*,
Copenhagen, 1849

This translation first published 1989
Reprinted with a new Chronology and Further Reading 2004
22

Translation, Editorial material copyright © Alastair Hannay, 1989, 2004
All rights reserved

Printed in England by Clays Ltd, St Ives plc
Filmset in Meridien (Linotron 202)

ISBN-13: 978-0-140-44533-6

CONTENTS

Translator's Note   vii
Introduction   1

THE SICKNESS UNTO DEATH   33
Preface   35
Introduction   37

PART ONE   41
The Sickness unto Death is Despair

PART TWO   107
Despair is Sin

Notes   167
Chronology   180
Further Reading   187

TRANSLATOR'S NOTE

The translation is based on the third and current edition of Kierkegaard's *Samlede Værker* (Gyldendal, Copenhagen, 1963) with minor corrections to be found in the Inter Editions (Montreal) machine-readable version of the Danish text. The end-notes are in part based on those of the editors of the 1963 edition, but contain significant expansions and additions.

INTRODUCTION

The biggest danger, that of losing oneself, can pass off in the world as quietly as if it were nothing; every other loss, an arm, a leg, five dollars, a wife, etc. is bound to be noticed.

Anti-Climacus*

A sickness 'unto death' would normally be an illness that someone took with them to the grave, or more pointedly the one that *took them* there. In the New Testament story, Jesus raised Lazarus from the dead, thereby showing that Lazarus's own sickness unto death was miraculously now no longer so – though of course in the end Lazarus presumably died like everyone else. But such fatal, or 'terminal', illness is not what Kierkegaard's title refers to. As the author points out in his Introduction, there is a sense in which, even if Jesus had not raised Lazarus from the dead, the story implies that neither his nor anyone else's sickness is 'unto death'. For in that story Jesus is Christ, and Christ is 'the resurrection and the life'; so for the Christian, that is to say, for the person who believes that the historical Jesus was Christ, the Lord's anointed, nothing human that ends in death comes thereby to an end. There is everlasting life.

The 'sickness' which Kierkegaard's book refers to as 'unto death' is resistance to this belief. It is the inclination to accept that as far as the individual is concerned, death is indeed the end. Now why should Kierkegaard want to call that a sickness? After all, even in his own time there must have been people

* See pp. 62–3 below.

1

strong both in mind and body who rejected the Christian teaching of sin and salvation, and who faced what they accepted as total extinction with equanimity. And today, of course, even in societies that once proudly professed Christian principles, the rejection of Christian belief – or at least the failure unequivocally to accept it – is the rule rather than the exception. So in what sense can the denial of Christian dogma constitute an illness?

The aim of my Introduction is to bring out background considerations which may help readers unfamiliar with Kierkegaard's writings to answer this question for themselves. It may be useful at the outset to divide the question into two by asking first: In what sense does Kierkegaard mean the failure of Christian faith to be a sickness unto death? And second: Has the diagnosis any plausibility? As will be apparent, answering the first question goes quite a long way towards answering the second. Although no really satisfactory answers may be available, raising the questions should in any case help the reader to grasp the plan and potential impact of this remarkable book. Having discussed them I shall add some comments helping to situate the book in the context of the life and work of its equally remarkable author.

In its widest sense a sickness is a disturbance in what would otherwise be a state of general well-being. The disorder might be physical or mental. The sickness which is the topic of Kierkegaard's work is mental, though it is important to note that Kierkegaard actually describes it as a sickness of the 'spirit'. To us mental illness is a familiar enough idea, very much more so than to Kierkegaard's readers almost a hundred and fifty years ago. But what normally leads one to accept the categorization of a mental disturbance as 'sickness' is the assumption that its immediate cause is something outside the patient's control, as in mumps (whether or not you deliberately invite contagion), and that its subsequent history is determined by specific tendencies to chronicity, malignancy or return to health inherent in the particular disease itself. What Kierkegaard refers to as the sickness unto death, however, is a disturbance the persistence, aggravation and removal of which are matters of the patient's own personal choice. One is responsible for 'catching' the illness and according to Kierkegaard its persistence is due to one's constantly continuing to 'catch' it.

That, however, would be too bald an account. Certainly the forms of the 'sickness' that the book ends up by stressing most are those in which the option of 'health' is consciously rejected; eventually, if allowed to run its course, the sickness comes to a crisis in the form of a choice between well-being (or salvation) and a fully conscious rejection of Christian teaching as 'untruth and a lie'. But the work as a whole (described as expository by its author) outlines in detail a morbid step-by-step progression towards this crisis from a state in which the sufferer is not even aware of the sickness, and where, of course, the sickness cannot be said to be maintained due to anything like a deliberate failure to choose health. In fact the principal theme of *The Sickness unto Death* is the raising of the level of a person's awareness of the urgency of the choice. Once the choice is clear, failure to follow Christian teaching is a matter of deliberate refusal or defiance. The subtitle identifies the work as a psychological exposition with Christianity as its background and as intended for 'edification and awakening'.

The psychology here is far removed from the behavioural science which goes by that name nowadays. Essentially, it is a form of phenomenological psychology, that is to say, a psychology which seeks confirmation in subjective experience of the truth of its descriptions of our mental states and of the ways these relate to, or unfold from, one another. On the other hand, because the work presupposes the Christian teaching of sin and redemption, it does not appeal to subjective experience alone. What Kierkegaard seems initially to be aiming at is recognition on the part of people who already profess Christian belief in some more or less habitual way, of the varying extents to which their lives constitute failures to measure up to the standards of what they profess, such failures in fact being timid

3

refusals to face the spiritual challenges of their alleged belief.

This fear is an essential element in Kierkegaard's portrayal or diagnosis of the lives and society of his contemporaries. In *The Concept of Dread* (also translated as 'The Concept of Anxiety')* published five years earlier, Kierkegaard describes 'spirit' in a human being as emerging from a state of innocence in which human fulfilment is regarded simply as development of human nature. 'Spirit' for Kierkegaard is what sets a human being apart from and above its simply human nature – apart from and above it in a way that leaves the individual without a given or natural identity, and forced to acknowledge or construct another. In *The Sickness unto Death* spirit is identified as the 'self', and we find that the increased levels of awareness which form the main topic of the 'exposition' are levels of an increasing *self*-awareness. Kierkegaard detects in contemporary life-styles, in the kinds of goals people set for themselves, in their ideals of fulfilment, a fundamental fear of conscious selfhood. He calls it 'despair'. And this, although it is also identified later as 'sin', is the most general designation of the 'sickness unto death'. The most common forms of despair are naturally enough those where the defences against conscious selfhood are most effectively deployed, and where the level of self-awareness is correspondingly low. Here, in greater or less degree, people are unconscious of their despair. However, Kierkegaard's exposition carries us beyond this defensive and (in his terms) unselfconscious response to emergent spirituality, and presents it as a stage in a malignant development which culminates in the 'demonic' denial of 'everything Christian: sin, the forgiveness of sins, etc.'. Such defiance is the 'height' of despair.

This raises several points which give us the opportunity to probe more deeply into the distinctive meaning of Kierkegaard's text.

* *The Concept of Dread*, tr. W. Lowrie (with intro. and notes), Princeton University Press, Princeton, NJ, 1944; and *The Concept of Anxiety*, ed. and tr. R. Thomte (with intro. and notes), Princeton University Press, Princeton, NJ, 1980.

Desirability of the Sickness

Let us begin by noting that the analogy with sickness, and with physical illness in particular, would normally suggest that once there is a cure for it, it can be applied at any stage, and the earlier the better. There may be illnesses that for various reasons are best left to run their course, but in general the ideal way to cope with an illness is to nip it in the bud. It is better still, of course, to take precautionary measures which prevent it occurring at all. But for Kierkegaard this analogy does not hold in the case of despair. Despair is not a disorder of the kind that should be rooted out or prevented. Indeed, from the point of view of spiritual development, there is something healthy about it. For one thing, even if it is clearly negative, despair is at least a sign of some first inkling of the requirements of such a development. But more than that, Kierkegaard thinks despair offers the only avenue to 'truth and deliverance'. This is an extremely important point, for it seems to imply that human development, spiritual development, is bound to progress through a state of sickness. The possibility of despair, we are told, is 'man's advantage over the beast' and 'the Christian's advantage over natural man'. Spiritual fulfilment requires that there be this possibility in order that despair be actively countered and 'rendered impotent'. To be cured is 'the Christian's blessedness'. The only way of escaping despair, therefore, seems to be to go through with it. The cure is for the self to 'found itself transparently in the power which established it', but since transparency here requires full self-awareness (in a sense to be discussed briefly in a moment), and full awareness of the self is the goal of spiritual development, the cure is simply not available until one reaches the point where continued denial of one's dependence upon God is an act of open defiance. Only then does the alternative – open acknowledgement of that dependence – become possible.

That does not, of course, preclude a person's reaching that

stage in a spirit of Christian acceptance rather than denial. And as far as that goes, the process of progressive self-awareness is also one which can be undergone by someone who, at least in his or her own eyes, has been a Christian all the way from childhood. But the only thing that conclusively establishes that there is no remnant of despair is this 'transparent' acknowledgement of individual dependence upon God, and it is clear that Kierkegaard considers the kind of professions that Christians typically make of their belief to fall well below that standard. These people, too, professed believers, are in despair, for they are denying themselves true selfhood. The important thing here, then, is that the progression is not described in terms of whether a person is willing or unwilling to profess belief in God (and Christ), but in terms of whether they are willing or unwilling to accept, and try to measure up to, a divinely set standard of human fulfilment. The author ironically chides his own society for its excessive humility, for having too low an ideal of fulfilment, while at the same time being conceited enough to think that measuring up to that modest ideal gives grounds for self-satisfaction. Among the forms of heightening despair that he describes, there is one which seems to have no progressive possibilities. This is a spiritual backwater which Kierkegaard calls 'spiritlessness', the protective absence of any consciousness of oneself as spirit. All despair, he says, is a 'negativity', but ignorance of it is a 'new negativity', and while one must 'pass through every negativity' to 'arrive at the truth', once in this backwater one has to paddle (or be propelled) back to where the current is, so that the progression to truth through all the other negativities can continue.

There is no doubt that Kierkegaard saw his own mission as a writer as that of assisting his readers to the consciousness of their own despair. And it is equally clear that he saw the progression to 'spirit' as one that requires the facing rather than the shelving of inherent difficulties. A note in his journals even sounds as though the encounter with difficulty must be enforced on one if one is to come further: 'He who has not suffered under human bestiality will not become spirit.'*

Pure Selfhood

It is clear from the above that the concept of selfhood in *The Sickness unto Death* must be a rather special one. Of course, the very notion of a self is vague, and it is impossible to assign it a definitive sense. So there may be nothing inherently peculiar or objectionable about the special sense employed by Kierkegaard. But if one starts with a very modest concept of selfhood, say one where being a self requires nothing more than the ability to answer to one's name, then Kierkegaard's concept is at least an extraordinarily immodest one. It requires that one answers directly to God.

Now that is not quite correct. In the first place, Kierkegaard talks of degrees of selfhood. Answering to God, or standing 'before' God, is the highest degree; but one can be less or more of a self, depending on the degree of one's self-consciousness. Again, this does not mean that there is a self already there, full-blown, of which one is more or less conscious of being; what Kierkegaard means is that the self is a less or a more full-blown self according to the person's consciousness of being a self. Selfhood is constituted *in* consciousness; it is itself, if you like, a kind and degree of consciousness: the kind that answers to eternal demands of an ethical nature, and the degree that corresponds to the clarity with which it grasps that it is of that kind. But also, second, Kierkegaard does not say that the highest degree of selfhood corresponds only to the paradigm of a person's answering to God; one can be as much of a self as it is possible to be and yet not answer to God. The requirement is that at least one have the 'conception' of God: 'The more conception of God, the more self' and vice versa. But you can

* *Søren Kierkegaards Papirer* (20 vols.), Gyldendal, Copenhagen, 1909–48, XI¹, A 407, p. 313.

have the conception of God and still not answer to him. You can have the conception of God and be 'before' God, or you can have the conception of God and have your back turned to God, or be standing at a distance disparaging all that God stands for.

But even possession of the conception of God is an extraordinarily strong requirement of selfhood, and the question it raises is, what justification is there for setting one's ideals of selfhood that high? Is it perhaps not simply that Kierkegaard imposes his Christian requirement quite arbitrarily, and that the consequent expanding of the range of sickness to cover what would normally be considered conditions of tolerable well-being, is merely ideologically motivated? Is it perhaps not also the case that Kierkegaard is guilty of confusing selfhood, as a certain kind of personal autonomy and consistency, with some other quite distinct notion of human fulfilment? Why, in any case, if selfhood is to be linked to fulfilment, should the fulfilment be specifically Christian?

Let us go back to a journal entry from two years prior to the publication of *The Sickness unto Death*. There Kierkegaard writes that 'the whole development of the world tends in the direction of the absolute significance of the category of particularity'.* Now that might be a prophetic or just a very discerning remark. It says that there are forces at work in history and society which place increasing and – when projected – absolute emphasis on sheer oneness, not the oneness of unity with others, but of singleness, particularity. The massive industrialization of European society in the nineteenth century led, as commentators have endlessly pointed out, to an atomization of the old, rurally based societies, with their organic groupings each with its clearly identified function. The age of 'rationalization' (to use Max Weber's terms) was one of 'disenchantment' (*Entzauberung*), a draining away of the ethical content that attached to membership, by virtue of one's well-defined group, in a large, coherent community, and the 'rational' reorganization of so-

---

* *Søren Kierkegaards Papirer*, VIII[1], A 9, p. 8.

ciety into a system of extreme division of labour, with consequent loss of corporate identity, multiple social roles, partition between social and personal identities, and so on. In this sense it is indeed true that Kierkegaard's world was bound for an absolutization of the particular, away from the universal. It is tempting, and not necessarily altogether misconceived, to bear this socio-economic development in mind when reading Kierkegaard's further remark that particularity is 'precisely the principle of Christianity'. What this suggests is that the exigencies of this develpment force upon people that state of particularity where, divested of any coherent social identity, they find themselves in the lonely situation that enables them, as single human beings, to stand directly before God.

To the critical reader, however, that situation has a twofold ambiguity. In the first place, standing before God in this way may simply accentuate the split between social and personal life. May not the self one is in standing before God, and which transcends one's fragile social ego, perhaps simply be a substitute for the self one can no longer 'put together' in social life? Or can standing before God be construed as a privileged situation which no merely socially constructed identities can provide, and which, furthermore, all attempts to establish such identities must merely frustrate? Secondly, as the former alternative indicates, there can be doubt about the status of the situation itself. Might not the idea that one can have an identity over and above whatever status one's social or familial roles, or the eyes of one's fellows, confer on one be altogether illusory? The God one stands before may be nothing more than a compensatory fiction, a factitious super-eye created to confer a specious status immune to the disintegrative tendencies at work in a modern society. Or, again, can it be that we do have eternal identities, which modern societies help us by default to find, by extruding us?

The former options have had their prophets too. For Kierkegaard, however, if we can adapt his remarks to these socio-economic circumstances, it is clearly the positive ones that apply. The more one loses any social identity, and the more naked, undifferentiated and 'spiritual' one becomes, the better adapted one is to occupy that solitary position 'directly before God'. And there is absolutely no suggestion that there is no God there to stand before. On the contrary, and this is something we shall briefly touch on below, according to *The Sickness unto Death* the suggestion would itself be a *sin*, the sin of rejecting Christianity as lies and falsehood, a sin which is despair at its height. The negative options are excluded by definition.

Whatever one's conclusions about that, there is no question that Kierkegaard's conception of selfhood fits the bill as far as the absolutization of particularity, or of individuality, is concerned. And one might argue that for any view of life at all in which individuality is put in the centre, Kierkegaard's self would be paradigmatic. That might even be argued in the case of a view in which individuality took the form of a socially conspicuous individualism, for such individualism is always comparative. You are an individualist because nobody does, or very few do, just the kinds of things you do, or does them in just your kind of way. But it is impossible to make such comparisons in the case of Kierkegaard's individual: its individuality is pure particularity; no comparisons with other individuals count at that level. When one stands there as Kierkegaard's individual one stands there bared of any basis for comparative identity and ready to found one's identity on something quite different. One is then, it could be said, a paradigmatic individual. This also indicates how the fact that Kierkegaard defines selfhood in terms of a conception of God may be understood. So long as it is assumed that identity is conferred in the eyes of another, God is the only resort for an individual for whom no intercomparative identity counts.

Reluctance and Refusal

There are two main, though not mutually irreducible, forms of despair in *The Sickness unto Death*. One is the despair of a person for whom the situation of the solitary individual is too strenuous an ideal. The other is the despair of a person who actively rejects the ideal. They are respectively called the despairs of not wanting to be oneself and of wanting to be oneself.* This sounds rather confusing, as though there could be no alternative to despair: whether you don't want to be yourself or you do, you are in despair. However, the despair of 'wanting to be oneself' is really that of wanting to be the self one is in one's own eyes and not those of God. It is wanting to be one's *own* self, instead of a self whose specifications and identity are the outcome of one's relationship to God. So the picture Kierkegaard presents of despair has these two forms: first, a reluctance to make headway towards the ideal of selfhood, a reluctance which also involves a more or less conscious fudging of the nature of the ideal and so also of the despairer's actual distance from it; and second, once the true nature of the ideal breaks through (once, as Kierkegaard puts it, there is 'consciousness of an infinite self'), a progressively clear-minded and deliberate refusal to accept it. In each of these phrases we are to assume that the ideal – the true self – is a self that conforms to the image of humanity revealed by God in the person of Christ.

There are plenty of reasons why there should be this reluctance and this refusal, even if we abide by the general assumption that Christianity provides the paradigm of selfhood. Of course, one's reluctance may stem simply and directly from disbelief in that assumption; and the question then is whether Kierkegaard or his pseudonym have anything to say to this kind

---

* Translators commonly use the form 'not to will to be oneself' and 'to will to be oneself'. But there is no need to use this archaic form and the Danish translates naturally and colloquially into 'not to want' and 'to want'.

of reluctance other than that from what they depict as the Christian point of view it is despair and sin.

Leaving that aside here, other reasons for reluctance and refusal have already been offered. One is that Kierkegaard's notion of selfhood requires a severing of the idea of oneself as a creature of one's role and reputation in human society, and acceptance of some identity for which all of that doesn't count. Another is the offence to reason presented in the reading of the Christian doctrine of the incarnation on which the ideal of selfhood is based. In *Concluding Unscientific Postscript** the whole idea that the eternal should enter time is described as a contradiction and 'inaccessible to thought'. On top of that comes the additional absurdity that in performing this inconceivable feat, God should also take on the form of a lowly servant, the least of mankind (in *Philosophical Fragments* the total unreasonableness of the doctrine is referred to as the 'absolute paradox'). Thus not only is no support for the ideal self forthcoming from the side of reason, but anything that might come from that direction shrieks out against it. There is, however, a further, perhaps more personally compelling reason for reluctance and refusal. Although Kierkegaard's concept of the self absolutizes the notion of selfhood, the absolutized self that eventually stands before God (and that must mean before Christ) hardly answers to the description of absolute selfhood that immediately leaps to the mind in an age that, at least in evaluative terms, associates selfhood with the achievement of a certain personal independence and self-centred autonomy. The self that stands before God has as its ideal or model a paradigm of *un*selfishness, of self*less*-ness. Whether this requirement is a logical consequence of the outlined notion of absolute individuality is unclear. Why should the God one stands before not demand self-assertion, self-glorification? Might perhaps the model offered in an alternative incarnation of the eternal have been one of outright selfishness? Or is that precluded somehow by the fact that it is the

---

* *Concluding Unscientific Postscript*, tr. D. F. Swenson and W. Lowrie, Princeton University Press, Princeton, NJ, 1941, p. 508.

eternal that is incarnated? Or even by the fact that the self *submits* to the model, whatever kinds of actions it presents as paradigmatic, that is even if it acts 'selfishly' out of a pure desire to follow the model? These are deep, though important, questions we cannot go into here, beyond remarking that in Kierkegaard's non-pseudonymous works we find the idea that acting in the way of the 'eternal' is acting for the good without thinking of one's own benefit, and without even thinking of the importance of one's *own* role in bringing the good about.* At least we can understand why people should be reluctant to become selves of this order, and why, when they realize what sort of self it is, they prefer to manufacture their own identities.

Unable to Die

But a person manufactures his or her own identity in vain. And this is a central feature of Kierkegaard's account of despair. When you manufacture your own identity, choose, construct and pursue your own ideal of human fulfilment, something essential is missing. Something that would prevent you simply demolishing the ideal and beginning all over again with a new ideal when the fancy takes you. Kierkegaard's text doesn't state directly what that is, beyond saying that such a person lacks something 'eternally firm'. It seems clear that the firmness cannot be part of what is chosen, a kind of gloss on the choice; that is, you will not achieve eternal firmness simply by saying 'I choose to be ideally thus, and also to be eternally firm in this choice,' for there is no reason why the latter constituent should be any the less instantly revocable than the former. Nor, it seems, would it be any better a proposal to say that someone who chooses to accept an identity in the eyes of God is, in effect, choosing something that is eternally firm by definition. For the fact that what you choose is eternally firm does not guarantee

---

* Cf. *Purity of Heart is to Will One Thing*, tr. (with intro.) D. V. Steere, Harper Torchbooks, New York, 1958.

that the choice of it will be equally so. Perhaps the answer lies in the thought that in the background of any such fundamental choice – and choosing how to specify oneself *qua* human being is pretty fundamental – there must be an indefeasible assumption of some kind which is, as such, even more fundamental, so fundamental that it could not be said to be chosen. It might, for example, be the assumption that life is meaningful, that there is at least some point of view from which the world makes sense; or it could be that God exists, or that God is Love. What is thus indefeasible would no doubt vary considerably from time to time and place to place, though by its very nature less from person to person. But for any such assumption, no conscious choice that goes against it, however fundamental, will be eternally firm, and any fundamental choice that is not so backed will be – well why not say it? – eternally unfirm. As Kierkegaard says, a person who chooses his own identity is 'a king without a country' and his subjects live in conditions where rebellion is 'legitimate at every moment'. Someone who has chosen to stand before God, on the other hand, knows that if he rebels, God is still there to judge him.

This would help to account for what must first strike the critical reader as a distinctly unsatisfactory aspect of Kierkegaard's 'exposition'. In *The Sickness unto Death* no allowance is made for the possibility that Christianity is indeed lies and falsehood. To reject Christianity as lies and falsehood, according to its author, is sin; in other words, rejecting the doctrine of sin and forgiveness is itself a sin, and indeed the greatest sin of all.

But there could also be a more superficial reason for this. The author of *The Sickness unto Death* is not given as Søren Kierkegaard himself, but as Anti-Climacus, with 'S. Kierkegaard' responsible for publication. Indeed the majority of Kierkegaard's best-known works, and all those of an 'expository' nature, are pseudonymous, for reasons Kierkegaard himself later explained. One reason was his wish to dissociate himself, at least in his reader's mind, from the views expressed in these works. This does not imply that in no case are the views or

14

attitudes expressed his own, but in this particular case we have Kierkegaard's own word that there is indeed a discrepancy between his own position and that of his pseudonym. Of his own relation to Anti-Climacus and to Johannes Climacus (the pseudonymous author of *Philosophical Fragments* and *Concluding Unscientific Postscript*) Kierkegaard wrote in his journal:

> J. Climacus has much in common with Anti-Climacus. But the difference is that while J. Climacus places himself so low that he even admits to not being a Christian, Anti-Climacus gives the impression of taking himself to be a Christian to an extraordinary degree, occasionally even of taking Christianity only to be for demons, though not in an intellectual respect . . . He has himself to blame for conflating himself with ideality (this is the demonic element in him), but his account of the ideality can be quite true, and I bow to it . . . I put myself higher than J. Climacus, lower than Anti-Climacus.*

The superficial reason for the absence of a genuinely nihilistic alternative in this work, then, is that its pseudonymous author is a Christian and the work is committed to the framework of Christian belief. For Anti-Climacus the life of spirit is one for which the relationship to God – standing before God – is presumptively valid from the start, simply because that is what the view he expresses dictates. No wonder, then, that everything else is despair and that there is no room in *The Sickness unto Death* for rejecting the Christian framework without this being judged a 'sin'; that is, without the rejection being understood in the very terms that are rejected.

This merely classificatory reason appears, however, unsatisfactory. Even though Anti-Climacus is made to say what Kierkegaard could not in all honesty say himself, the exercise of making him say it can hardly be dismissed as merely intellectual. It seems more likely that Anti-Climacus is used to present in ideal form a background assumption which for Kierkegaard himself was indefeasible, but which, once expressed in this way, he would reasonably find himself falling

* *Søren Kierkegaard's Papirer*, X¹, A 517, p. 332.

short of. Perhaps even inevitably, because perhaps any normal human being – as opposed to a demon, which as we know is a divine being though of an inferior sort* – would fall short.

That brings to mind Jean-Paul Sartre's famous pronouncement towards the close of *Being and Nothingness* that man is a 'useless passion'.† But there is a more interesting reverse parallel. The despair Anti-Climacus discusses as the 'sickness unto death' is either failure or refusal to place oneself in God's hands. And what makes the failure or refusal a state or an act of despair is that it involves a surrendering of the hope of reaching the goal of fulfilment. To despair is to give up hope. (Whereas to be desperate, or act desperately, on the other hand, is to act in the last extremity of hope.) Sartre maintains that human behaviour is based on a fundamental and indefeasible desire to be God, but the structure of human consciousness ensures that the desire (as also the notion of God) is contradictory. Being God is, of course, a very different goal from being placed in God's hands, and the difference suggests something of the distance that separates Kierkegaard from our own, post-Nietzschean culture. But there is a further twist to the difference. For although Anti-Climacus might be willing to describe his version of the goal of fulfilment as a fundamental passion, *he* would not describe it as a useless one. On the contrary, in impressing upon his readers that it is the only way out of despair, he must be assumed to imply that it is also a possible way out, in spite of the contradictory nature of the required belief that one is standing before God (Christ). What for Anti-Climacus is useless is the attempt to dislodge this fundamental 'passion' to rest in God, to

---

* Kierkegaard's remark about the demonic aspect of Anti-Climacus might be interpreted not just as saying that the ideal is super-human, but that in representing it as such, Anti-Climacus is in fact doing the devil's errand by making it appear *untrue* to human life and therefore to be rejected. This would accord with Anti-Climacus's own use of the term 'demonic' in the work, but sounds very like the form of despair Anti-Climacus himself calls the despair of infinitude.

† J.-P. Sartre, *Being and Nothingness*, tr. H. E. Barnes, Philosophical Library, New York, 1956, p. 615.

hinder this drive towards selfhood before God. Any attempt to do so will fail; that is to say, any attempt to get rid of this drive, to have *it* die, is in vain. And vain, too, as Kierkegaard characteristically points out, is any attempt to dispose of the self that is unable to eradicate this drive to die, and so too any attempt to dispose of the self that cannot rid itself of that incapable self, and so on. The 'torment of despair', says Anti-Climacus, 'is precisely not being able to die'. The despairer has his sickness unto death. It is despair that is the useless passion; it tries to but cannot 'consume the eternal'.

Readers of Sartre will notice one more twist. In taking the desire to be God as fundamental, Sartre is offering a diagnosis or explanation of behaviour which, if he were to use Kierkegaard's terminology, he would have to describe as despair. Sartre calls it *mauvaise foi*, or bad faith. People try to objectify themselves, to make themselves into substantial entities with built-in functions and values, thus denying the radical freedom that belongs to them by virtue of their being conscious. It is this that is the attempt to be God, who is both conscious (free) and substantial. A deep urge on the part of human beings to be complete in the way God is conceived as being is psychologically understandable. But the passion that drives those in 'bad faith' uselessly in quest of a divine nature is precisely a form of despair; it is an attempt to be rid of inherent deficiencies of the human state. For Anti-Climacus, on the other hand, despair is an attempt not to appropriate but to expunge the goal of completeness, which for him is the direction in which both deep passion and true selfhood lie.

Spiritual Need

But does human passion really lie in that direction? Or rather, is there an unexpungeable human yearning to occupy the position that Christianity provides, a place in which one's lot is to sin and one's expectations centre upon forgiveness and a consequent state of bliss? You would not think so. Indeed, some make so bold as to suggest that no one in their right mind would willingly conceive their life-situation in this light.

And yet if there is, as Anti-Climacus claims, a religious need which emerges through a heightened awareness of oneself, and if Christianity offered the only possible scenario for satisfying that need, then there would certainly be something to it. Indeed, if one were able to show that Kierkegaard has unearthed a universal spiritual need, *The Sickness unto Death* would be immediately topical.

Now many people, though not perhaps the habitual Christians whom Kierkegaard castigates, might agree at least to the extent of allowing that Kierkegaard has discovered that need in himself. They may even agree that the need in question was not altogether untypical of certain kinds of people with certain kinds of background. Something like this is expressed by Ludwig Wittgenstein when he remarks that the Christian religion 'is only for the man who needs infinite help, that is, for the man who experiences infinite torment', and that, as he sees it, 'the Christian faith . . . is a man's refuge in this *ultimate* torment'.*

The modern way with such needs would be to prevent them occurring, as if they were disorders on a par with physical ailments. Religious solutions to human misery are often seen as makeshifts awaiting genuine amelioration through some beneficial adjustment in the conditions of life. But it is also possible to look at it the other way around. One may always, of course, give psychological and sociological explanations of why people like Kierkegaard have such needs. But one may also choose to side with Kierkegaard, to see things as he does, and say, 'This is how it really is.' What is exceptional about people like Kierkegaard might be not so much that they are in the unfortunate position

---

* L. Wittgenstein, *Culture and Value*, tr. P. Winch, Blackwell, Oxford, 1980, p. 46e. The word translated 'torment' (*Not*) includes the sense of 'need'. The passage also contains the remark: 'The whole planet can suffer no greater torment than a *single* [*eine*] soul.' Wittgenstein was an admirer of Kierkegaard.

of having to contend with this special problem, but that they are in the unusual position of being able to see that there is this problem. It is not necessary to regard the special circumstances in which the need arises as inducing some kind of emotional distortion; they can equally be described as dispersing the clouds of confusion by which people normally contrive to obscure from themselves the realities of their situation. In this sense, one may even choose to regard Kierkegaard as 'enjoying' a kind of privileged access to a universal problem to which the vast majority remain blind.

There is a residual difficulty with what seems to be an assumption here, namely that where there is a problem there must be a solution. Even if you are disposed to agree about there being this religious need, perhaps also agreeing that it might be universal, there is no compulsion for you to accept the Christian scenario as a solution, even if it were the only one available. There is indeed a problem with the whole idea of believing something because one wants to rather than because the evidence pushes one in that direction.* It sounds like wishful thinking. On the other hand, in reading Kierkegaard it is hard to make the words 'wishful thinking' fit easily with the suffering that he believes to be attendant upon and indeed induced through one's acceptance of Christian teaching. And some of the nub of the problem might disappear if the motivation for retaining the teaching, having first accepted it, were not whatever led one to choose it in the first place – for example, the prospect of eternal bliss – but the fact that, along with the attendant hardships, it provided better opportunities for living one's life as an authentic individual.

---

* See Bernard Williams, 'Deciding to Believe', in *Problems of the Self*, Cambridge University Press, Cambridge, 1973, pp. 136–51.

Structure of the Self

It is important when reading *The Sickness unto Death* to take its philosophical terminology seriously, that is, literally, at least as far as the literal meanings are textually identifiable. Kierkegaard takes his reader in at the deep end. The first three paragraphs are a concentrate of the book's philosophical vocabulary. Indeed, if one reads these paragraphs as a sample of what to expect in the body of the discussion, it is quite likely the book would be back on the shelf in no time. Some commentators have even suggested that the passage in question is a parody of the impenetrability of Hegelian prose. But that is clearly mistaken. These early lines function as a table of contents; they present the scope of the discussion and its conceptual apparatus in the most succinct possible way. The problem for contemporary readers, however, is that the terms used are no longer as current as they once were. Many contemporary commentators have fallen for the temptation of translating them into a more modern idiom, giving them meanings which they think allow Kierkegaard's insights to stand up and be counted in the market of contemporary ideas. The result is often to trivialize the insights and to leave the misleading impression that their expressions are just borrowings from the idioms available in his time.

The reader has to identify and connect two principal components in Kierkegaard's account of despair. The first is a set of oppositions, three in number though one of them has to be looked at apart. The three are 'infinite' and 'finite', 'eternal' and 'temporal' (in the opening passage these are unaccountably reversed), and 'freedom' (later 'possibility') and 'necessity'. The book starts off by saying that the human being is a 'synthesis' of these (let us call them) 'factors'. Apart from identifying the factors one wants to know what kind of connection, compilation, or whatever, this synthesis is supposed to be. The second main component of Kierkegaard's account of despair is an idea of the 'self', not as some kind of substance or thing, some entity which the human being ineluctably is, or assembles itself into being, but as a 'relation' which 'relates to itself'.* This self-relating relation, or self-relating synthesis, is what Kierkegaard calls 'spirit'.

Imbalance within the Self

Let us look first at the oppositions, or 'polarities' as they are sometimes called. The terms for the factors themselves have a long philosophical (and theological) tradition. If we begin with the two sets of polarities which go together, the oppositions between being *finite* and *infinite*, and between being *necessitated* and being *free*, oppose the idea of being limited or confined in some way, or ways, to that of being unlimited or unconfined in that or those ways. In the section 'The forms of this sickness', which gives what might be called his nosology of despair, Kierkegaard gives no very clear specification of what these ways are. But one gathers something from the general character-izations he gives of people who fail to preserve a 'healthy'

---

* Because the Danish for 'to relate' (in the sense of 'to be in relation') (*at forholde sig*) has a reflexive form, translators have rendered this 'relates itself to itself', which has then been construed as meaning 'relates its actual to its true self' (or vice versa). This is both unnecessary and misleading. The Danish says simply that to be a self is for the synthesis to have a relation to itself, that is, to be self-related. The distinction between an actual and a true self is already contained in that of the synthesis. That remark must none the less be qualified. The synthesis is also described in one place as simply 'psychophysi-cal', that is, as just a relation between mind and body. This refers, however, to the human synthesis prior to its relating to itself from the point of view of 'spirit'. To keep the picture consistent, one should perhaps construe the self-relation in a strong sense, such that the synthesis only relates to itself when it has enough of a self to bear a *self*-relation. And then the synthesis can be construed in terms of actual (imbalanced) and ideal (balanced) selves. A person without spirit must have enough reflexivity to carry on a spiritless existence. If one grants a weaker sense of 'relating to itself', one could say that it does not relate to itself as a self. Kierkegaard does not often pause to define his terms.

balance between them, though these characterizations do not include portrayals of the balanced state of 'health'. What we are given are abstract sketches of types of despair in which one or the other factor is given undue weight, or one factor takes over altogether. Thus, roughly, the whole emotional, cognitive and volitional life of a person who lives in the infinite without a counterbalance in the finite is given over to imagination; while a person who has nothing of the infinite lives a well-oiled but totally unimaginative everyday life. What is missing in either case is the opposition in which the healthy balance must be struck. For despair to disappear imagination must be applied to something specific, or, from the other side, everyday occupation must become the workplace of the imagination. Similarly, to have a freedom (though Kierkegaard now substitutes the term 'possibility' for 'freedom') not counterpoised by necessity is to treat all projects as though they were accomplished at the start; while to have nothing of the possible is to see oneself bound to a chain of ongoing events that leave no place for personal initiative. In respect of this polarity, the healthy balance is one in which time and trouble are duly taken in the realization of possibilities, in the light of the historical, genetic and social conditions which govern the gap from possibility to actuality; or, from the other side, in which this 'facticity' is not allowed to dictate what is possible.

As noted above, the third polarity (though second in the list given initially) – *eternal* and *temporal* – has to be treated apart. It provides the framework for the third and longest part of the section on 'The forms of this sickness', and is linked to the process of growing self-awareness. To become aware of one's self is to become aware, at the same time, of 'something eternal' in the self, and we are to take this to mean that in some sense the self transcends the temporal sphere in which its existence is none the less rooted. It is not clear how we are to understand this 'something eternal'. But generally in Kierkegaard's writings the eternal represents a goal of human endeavour, a fundamental goal, on a par with Sartre's 'useless passion', though from Anti-Climacus's viewpoint not useless even though contradictory. Perhaps one might even describe the eternal as the interest that motivates one to *become* a self. Elsewhere it is described as 'peacefulness',* which suggests a state of well-being, though perhaps an eternal state of the temporal mind rather than timeless peace in the afterlife, since it is also identified as 'oneself' taken as 'the object of seriousness',† and becoming a self is a project that occurs in time, that is in finite, necessitated circumstances.

Above I remarked that there has been a tendency among contemporary commentators to give these distinctions meanings for which the traditional terminology employed by Kierkegaard is not essential. Thus one finds the infinite/finite and possibility/necessity polarities treated as though they were both (indistinguishably) simply the distinction between possibility in principle and possibility in practice. Thus the healthy balance is to do only what is possible in the circumstances in which you find yourself. That is obviously a gross trivialization of what anything close to a literal reading of the text would lead one to identify as its author's meaning. As the reader discovers, the positive factors in these two pairs (infinite/finite and possibility/necessity) are illustrated, respectively, by the notions of being in God's presence and of God's omnipotence. The clear indications are that the 'synthesis' of opposites is a relation between the human being's historically (etc.) given situation, his or her given workplace if you like, and the ideal of 'true' selfhood outlined above. The forms of the sickness of despair are then imbalances that fail to bring the historical and ideal together.

---

* *Søren Kierkegaard's Papirer*, X², A 617, p. 442.
† See *The Concept of Anxiety*, ed. and tr. R. Thomte (with intro. and notes), Princeton University Press, Princeton, NJ, 1980, pp. 150, 152 and 154.

Self-conscious Choice

The second main component of despair, as previously mentioned, is the idea of the self as a 'relation which relates to itself'. The relation itself is the synthesis, typically in some form of imbalance as above. Now what the eternal/temporal contrast enables us to see is how this relation-in-imbalance becomes progressively conscious of its being an imbalance and, more particularly, of its being an imbalance in accordance with the first two polarities. The more aware a person is of having an 'eternal' aspect, the clearer it becomes that these polarities *are* to be described as suggested above, that is, as already implying the goal of 'true' selfhood. When we ask now what the relation to *itself* is, which, according to the text, *is* the self, the obvious interpretation is that it is the *consciousness* of itself as a synthesis, typically in a state of imbalance. In other words the self is its consciousness of itself.

But what is self-consciousness? Being able to answer to one's name? Self-centredness and embarrassment? Introspection? One could focus, as Robert Burns in his words of comfort to the mouse, on the discomforting ability humans have to 'cast' their eye backward on 'prospects drear' and forward to what they cannot see but can 'guess and fear';* or perhaps on the strategic advantages possessed by beings who, unlike the less fortunate mouse, are 'touched' not only by 'the present'. But Kierkegaard's notion of self-consciousness is clearly moral. That is, it is neither merely introspective nor merely practical in the sense of strategic. What Kierkegaard's self is conscious of is itself as being in a state of despair, but also of itself as despair*ing*, as being responsible for failing to keep to its ideal of fulfilment, or failing to keep that ideal in view. This failure may take the form of a tendency to exclude the ideal and to live in the despairs of finitude or necessity (keeping hold of the temporal); or it may

---

* 'To a Mouse on Turning her up in her Nest with a Plough' (1785).

take the form of a tendency to live a double life in which the ideal is preserved but at a level where there seems no question of its being related to real life, or where the possibilities are treated as if they were realized without real life's intervention. In all these cases, one loses one's self, *is* losing one's self. But, as our motto says, this loss may well go unremarked in the world, while losing 'an arm, a leg, five dollars, a wife, etc. is bound to be noticed'.

What gives the self-relation its moral character is not that the self's possibilities are defined by some moral code which the self is then aware of not following. That would not amount to the self's task being that of becoming 'itself' as an individual before God. As Kierkegaard first indicated in *Fear and Trembling*, if the individual takes precedence over the group, it must acquire its moral 'code' directly from the eternal source of all value, while moral codes are in fact laid down in communities and the morality of actions is decided at a level more general than that of the individual. Kierkegaard's 'self' (or 'spirit') is aware of its situation in regard to its 'true' self: the degree to and the respects in which it is in despair, failing to measure up to its goal, trying to conceal from itself the fact that it is not measuring up; perhaps even trying – by lowering its aim – to conceal from itself the fact that it is trying to conceal that fact from itself, and so on, it seems without end.*

If this reading is correct – and the reader will be able to make up her or his own mind on that – then a very common interpretation of Kierkegaard will be wrong. He is often portrayed as originating the existentialist idea that man is a freely self-interpreting animal; that is, the idea that the one essential truth about human beings is that they can, indeed are compelled to, decide their own natures, for nothing is determined for them in this respect. One hears the notion of 'criterionless choice' in connection with Kierkegaard, as though what life-

---

* The idea of the self as a relation that 'relates to itself' is not original to Kierkegaard but is found in Hegel's *Phenomenology of Spirit*, tr. A. V. Miller, Clarendon Press, Oxford, 1979, p. 12.

view one chooses is wholly arbitrary because not founded on any determinable standard, the standard itself having to be chosen. *The Sickness unto Death* assumes a standard, and the crux of its account of despair is that one denies it at one's peril; while the book's message is that people are for the most part busily engaged in denying it. What Kierkegaard means by the choice of oneself (a notion central to the second part of *Either/Or*, but not found in so many words in *The Sickness unto Death*) is a decision to resort to a deep intuition about the true nature of selfhood, not an arbitrary selection from a cafeteria of alternatives. That would be to be a 'king without a country', itself a form of despair. The intuition to be resorted to is that the model of true selfhood is that offered in the example of Christ.* The choice to resort to it is in a way criterionless: there is nothing to provide conclusive justification of it, and indeed the whole notion of Christ – of God the eternal in time – is absurd. But the whole point of Kierkegaard's authorship, from *Philosophical Fragments* on, is to impress on his reader that in matters of this kind there can be no such justification, yet that this in turn is no reason for abstaining from choice.

Kierkegaard: Life and Works

The Sickness unto Death appeared in Reitzel's bookshop in Copenhagen on 30 July 1849. (It is worth noting that the archaic 'unto' in the English version of the title is due to the relevant passage of the Gospel according to St John in the English Authorized Version; the Danish Bible has the preposition *til* which is translated straightforwardly as 'to', though the archaic version has the advantage of preserving the rhythm of the ending of the Danish title, *Sygdommen til Døden*.) By that time Kierkegaard was thirty-six years old and the book proved

---

* As spelled out in a companion work *Indøvelse i Christendom* ('Practice in Christianity'), translated by W. Lowrie as *Training in Christianity*, Princeton University Press, Princeton, NJ, 1944, p. 109.

to be his penultimate major publication. A companion piece (*Practice in Christianity*) was published just over a year later. Kierkegaard died in 1855 aged forty-two with more than a dozen major works to his credit and a profusion of lesser writings and pamphlets.

Søren Aabye Kierkegaard (an earlier spelling of the Danish for 'churchyard', and carrying as in English the primary connotation of 'graveyard') was born in Copenhagen on 5 May 1813. His father's family had worked the land of their local priest in Jutland, in a feudal arrangement that gave them their name. The father himself was formally released from his virtual vassalage by the priest at the age of twenty-two, at a time when in practice he had already moved to Copenhagen to work in an uncle's hosiery business. Kierkegaard senior later inherited his uncle's fortune and became a wealthy wholesaler of imported goods on his own account, leaving a fair fortune to Søren on his death. Søren was the youngest of seven children whose mother was their father's second wife and formerly maid to the first, who, in 1794, died childless after two years of marriage. There was some scandal about the first child's date of birth. A brother and sister died before Søren was nine. His two surviving sisters, a brother and his mother all died not long before he was twenty-one, and Søren became convinced that he himself would not live to be more than thirty-three. He was educated at a strictly run School of Civic Virtue, gained there a reputation for a quick tongue and sharp wit, and then (after being discharged from the Royal Guards after only three days as unfit for duty) at Copenhagen University, where he enrolled in 1830. His chosen subject was theology, but he studied widely in the liberal arts and science as well, spending in all seven years as a student, his father footing the not inconsiderable bills.

The sequence of events which turned Kierkegaard to full-time authorship began in 1837 when he met Regine Olsen, daughter of a Copenhagen dignitary. Regine was then fourteen years old. The following year Kierkegaard's father died aged eighty-one (Kierkegaard was then twenty-five). The father had exercised a great and largely oppressive influence on the son from early childhood, and Kierkegaard, who later felt that he never enjoyed a proper childhood, had in the end found it necessary to try to recapture his spontaneity by breaking free from his father's hold. Two years before the meeting with Regine he had been describing Christianity, associated with his father, as a debilitating influence. He looked about him for some other idea 'to live or die for',* forsook his studies, and led outwardly the life of a rich young man about town, aesthete and wit. Entries in his journal, however, tell a different story. Kierkegaard was really undergoing a period of deep and even occasionally suicidal depression. Shortly before his father's death this period nevertheless culminated in a reconciliation between the two. The year of his father's death also saw his first book, *From the Papers of One Still Living*, and then two years later, on 10 September 1840, he became engaged to Regine, underwent practical training for a career in the State Church, and in 1841 published and publicly defended his doctoral thesis, *The Concept of Irony with Constant Reference to Socrates*. Having already preached his first sermon, Kierkegaard seemed all set for a life of civic virtue.

But that was not to be. Well before the end of that year, in August 1841, Kierkegaard had returned Regine's engagement ring. By November, not long after the defence of his thesis, the break became final and Kierkegaard was on his way for the first of what were to be four visits to Berlin, on this occasion attending Schelling's lectures there (at about the same time as Karl Marx, it is thought, though there is no record of their meeting). Whatever the private reasons for this turn of events, there followed a flood of pseudonymous works focusing first on the problem of entering into the life of a society ('realizing the universal'), a theme obviously now very close to Kierkegaard's

* The details of Kierkegaard's life are largely gathered from Josiah Thompson's excellently vivid biography, *Kierkegaard*, A. A. Knopf, New York, 1973. The account here is drawn from my own *Kierkegaard*, Routledge and Kegan Paul, London, 1982, ch. 1.

heart. In February 1843 *Either/Or* appeared (in two volumes, each of over 400 pages), followed in October by two slimmer volumes, *Repetition* and *Fear and Trembling** (both written on a second visit to Berlin, not long after the publication of *Either/ Or*). The same theme, though now with a distinctive religious aspect more in evidence, was pursued in the substantial *Stages on Life's Way*, published in April 1845. But already in June of the previous year there had appeared two books introducing new topics. *Philosophical Fragments* sought, in subtle and spare language, to offer a Christian alternative to Hegelian philosophy, though without mentioning the latter. The theme was elaborated more explicitly, at great length and with much humour, almost two years later in *Concluding Unscientific Postscript to the Philosophical Fragments*, a two-volume work in its Danish version. Within a few days of *Philosophical Fragments*, however, there had also appeared *The Concept of Dread* (alternatively 'The Concept of Anxiety'), an examination of the psychological background to the experience of sin and a work which anticipates *The Sickness unto Death*. Alongside this already impressive production, Kierkegaard also published twenty-one 'edifying' and 'Christian' discourses under his own name, some of them published simultaneously with works under pseudonyms.

Concluding Unscientific Postscript was to have been Kierkegaard's swansong as author. A few days before the manuscript of *Postscript* was delivered to the printer, Kierkegaard provoked a feud with a satiric periodical called *Corsair* (*Corsaren*) which then mercilessly caricatured him, his posture, clothes and unusual jerky gait. Three weeks before the publication of *Postscript*, and while the *Corsair* business was at its height, Kierkegaard wrote in his journal that he felt his time as an author was over, and even before the feud it appears he had given thought once more to the priesthood. There remained only one more literary chore – the proofreading of a review of a book called *Two Ages*, a

---

* Also published in Penguin Classics.

review in which he may have felt that he had rounded off his work by spelling out its social and political implications.

But by the beginning of the following year Kierkegaard was dismissing these plans as a lapse of nerve and the author was in full spate again. That same year (1847) he published *Edifying Discourses in Different Spirits* and the substantial *Works of Love*, followed in the spring of 1848 by *Christian Discourses* and in 1849 *The Lilies of the Field and the Birds of the Air* and *Three Discourses at Communion on Fridays*. There then followed the works of a new pseudonym, Anti-Climacus: *The Sickness unto Death* and *Practice in Christianity*.

These two works really form the coping-stones of the general world-view expressed in the earlier pseudonymous writings. But they are natural partners to the religious discourses among which they appeared (and more of which were to follow). They exploit the ambitious spiritual level of the discourses in order to cast new light on the themes of the earlier pseudonyms. *The Sickness unto Death* resumes the theme of Vigilius Haufniensis's *The Concept of Dread*, and *Practice in Christianity* that of *Philosophical Fragments*. In all these later works one may detect a new stringency. Perhaps the *Corsair* affair, which left Kierkegaard an object of public ridicule, enforced a polarization between him and his society. His own suffering for truth was set off against the complacency of a bourgeois public which manifested its self-contentment not least in the manner of its religious observances, and whose religious leaders, formerly close associates of Kierkegaard and friends of his family, struck him as exemplars of self-seeking worldliness. Thus, in a way, the social and political criticism that emerged in what might have been Kierkegaard's final work, the review of *Two Ages*, was a seed that developed in the atmosphere created by the feud with *Corsair* to become a general condemnation of the age in which he lived. *The Sickness unto Death* diagnoses the problem as despair, a two-sided problem to both sides of which his personal experience gave him exceptional access: the inner conflicts involved in becoming a self, and the outward manifestations in his contemporaries of failure to confront or even recognize these conflicts.

In the next few years Kierkegaard wrote little until unleashing a vitriolic attack on the State Church, which he now saw clearly as the real root and bastion of spiritual complacency and compromise. During these years he lived in increasingly straitened circumstances and the remainder of his inheritance and the modest proceeds of his authorship went to financing the final assault, among other things through the publication of his own broadsheet, *The Instant*. This went through nine issues before Kierkegaard fell ill, collapsed in the street, and died in hospital some six weeks later, probably of a lung infection. On his sick-bed he confided to Emil Boesen, his friend from boyhood – indeed by that time his only friend, now a pastor and the only member of the Church he would see, including his own brother – that his life had been a 'great and to others unknown and incomprehensible suffering', which looked like 'pride and vanity' but 'wasn't'. He regretted that he had not married and taken on an official position. Kierkegaard's funeral was the occasion of a minor disturbance led by one of his first supporters, a student nephew, who protested at the Church's insistence on officiating at the committal proceedings, contrary to the deceased's wishes. That Kierkegaard, however opposed to the Church, none the less believed his own physical sickness was not unto death is indicated by the inscription he had himself chosen for the gravestone:

> In yet a little while
> I shall have won;
> Then the whole fight
> Will at once be done.
> Then I may rest
> In bowers of roses
> And perpetually
> Speak with my Jesus.*

---

* From a hymn written by H. A. Brorson (1694–1764). See *S. Kierkegaard's Letters and Documents*, tr. H. Rosenmeier, Princeton University Press, Princeton, NJ, 1978, pp. 26–7.

As for the spiritual sickness, one may surmise how far Kierkegaard had himself experienced what he called this inability to die.*

* This introduction owes much to discussion with colleagues and the writings of Kierkegaard scholars, too many to be listed here. But I wish to record my debt particularly to Paul Dietrichson and to Gordon Marino. I would also like to thank Sarah Gustavus-Jones, my most perceptive copy editor at Penguin.

The Sickness unto Death

Lord! Give us weak eyes for
things of no account,
and eyes of full clarity
in all your truth[1]

PREFACE

The form of this 'exposition' may strike many readers as odd: to them it would seem too rigorous to be edifying and too edifying to have the rigour of scholarship. On the latter I have no opinion, but regarding the former I disagree, and were it indeed too rigorous to be edifying, I would consider that a fault. It is one thing, naturally, that not everyone will find it edifying; not everyone is qualified to respond to it in that way, but the fact that the work itself is edifying in character is something else. In a Christian context everything, yes everything, should serve to edify. The kind of scholarship that is not in the last resort edifying is for that very reason un-Christian. An account of anything Christian must be like a physician's lecture beside the sick-bed; even if only those skilled in the medical arts should understand it, it should never be forgotten where it is being given. It is just this relationship to life of whatever is Christian (contrasted with a scholarly remoteness), or this, the ethical side of Christianity, that edifies; and an account of this sort, whatever rigour it may possess, is quite different, even in kind, from the 'disinterested' scientific approach whose superior heroism is so far from being heroism in a Christian sense that in a Christian sense it is a form of inhuman curiosity. Christian heroism, and indeed one perhaps sees little enough of that, is to risk unreservedly being oneself, an individual human being, this specific individual human being alone before God, alone in this enormous exertion and this enormous accountability. But it is not Christian heroism to be taken in by the pure concept of humanity as such, or to have world-history play the admiration game.[2] All Christian knowledge, whatever formal rigour it betrays, should be concerned. But what edifies is just this concern. The concern is the relation to life, to what a person actually is, and thus, in a Christian sense, it is seriousness. In a Christian sense, the superior elevation of disinterested knowing, far from being greater seriousness, is frivolity and pretence. But again, what edifies is seriousness.

In one respect then, this little book is the sort a student might have written, but perhaps in another respect not just any professor.

But that the treatise is dressed up as it is is at least well-advised; yet I would also think psychologically appropriate. There's a more ceremonious style which is too ceremonious to be much to the point and which, to those all too familiar with it, easily becomes meaningless.

Just one more comment, doubtless superfluous but I'll risk that: I wish it to be known once and for all that in this entire work, as the title indeed indicates, despair is to be understood as the sickness, not the remedy.[3] Such is the dialectical nature of despair. So too in Christian terminology is death the expression for the greatest spiritual misery and yet the cure just to die, to depart from life.[4]

1848

INTRODUCTION

'This sickness is not unto death' (John 11.4). But still Lazarus died. Upon the disciples misunderstanding him when he later added: 'Our friend Lazarus sleepeth, but I go, that I may awake him out of sleep' (11.11), Christ told them bluntly: 'Lazarus is dead' (11.14). So Lazarus is dead, and yet this sickness was not unto death; he was dead, and still this sickness is not unto death. We know, of course, that Christ was thinking of the miracle which, 'if [they] wouldest believe', was to let contemporaries see 'the glory of God' (11.40), that miracle through which he awoke Lazarus from the dead; so 'this sickness' was not merely 'not unto death', but, as Christ had foretold, 'for the glory of God, that the son of God might be glorified thereby' (11.4). Ah!, but even had Christ not awoken Lazarus, is it not still true that this sickness, death itself, is not unto death? When Christ steps forward to the grave and in a loud voice cries out, 'Lazarus, come forth' (11.43), it is plain enough that *this* sickness is not unto death. Yet, even if Christ had not said that, doesn't simply the fact that He who is 'the resurrection and the life' (11.25) steps forward to the grave mean that this sickness is not unto death? That Christ exists – doesn't that mean that this sickness is not unto death? And what good would it have done Lazarus to be awoken from the dead if in the end he must die anyway? What good would it have done Lazarus if He did not exist, He who is the resurrection and the life for every person who believes in Him? No, it is not because Lazarus was awoken from the dead; that is not why we can say this sickness is not unto death. It is because He exists; that is why this sickness is not unto death. For in human terms death is the last thing of all, and in human terms hope exists only so long as there is life; but to Christian eyes death is by no means the last thing of all, just another minor event in that which is all, an eternal life. And to Christian eyes there is in death infinitely more hope than in, simply in human terms, not merely life itself but life at its height of health and vigour.

So to Christian eyes not even death is the 'sickness unto death', so much less so everything that goes under the name of earthly and temporal suffering: want, illness, misery, hardship, adversity, torment, mental agony, sorrow, grief. And even where these are so hard and painful that we humans, or at any rate the sufferer, would say that 'this is worse than death', to Christian eyes none of this, which even where it isn't in fact sickness is comparable to it, is the sickness unto death.

This then is the measure of the high-mindedness with which Christianity has taught the Christian to think of all that is worldly, death included. It's almost as if the Christian were supposed to vaunt this proud elevation above all that humanity normally calls misfortune, over what humanity normally calls the greatest evil. But then Christianity has discovered in its turn a misery which humanity as such does not know exists. This misery is the sickness unto death. What the natural man counts terrible, when it is all added up and he can think of no remainder, all this the Christian treats as a joke. Such is the relation between the natural man and the Christian; it is like that between a child and an adult: what the child shrinks from in horror the adult thinks nothing of. The child doesn't know what is horrifying; the adult knows, and he shrinks from it in horror. The child's imperfection is, first, not to know what is horrifying, and then by the same token to shrink from something else in horror. So too with the natural man. He has no knowledge of what is truly horrifying, yet is not exempted thereby from shrinking in horror. No, he shrinks in horror from what is not horrifying. It is something like the pagan's relationship to God: he doesn't know the true God, but as if that weren't enough he worships an idol as God.

Only the Christian knows what is meant by the sickness unto death. As a Christian he has acquired a courage unknown to the natural man, a courage he acquired by learning to fear something even more horrifying. That is always how a person acquires courage: when he fears a greater danger he always has the courage to face a lesser. When one fears a danger infinitely, it is as if the others weren't there at all. But the truly horrifying thing which the Christian has learned to know is the 'sickness unto death'.

Christian knows reality

PART ONE

The Sickness unto Death is Despair

A

Despair is a sickness of the spirit, of the self, and so can have three forms: being unconscious in despair of having a self (inauthentic despair), not wanting in despair to be oneself, and wanting in despair to be oneself

The human being is spirit. But what is spirit? Spirit is the self. But what is the self? The self is a relation which relates to itself, or that in the relation which is its relating to itself. The self is not the relation but the relation's relating to itself. A human being is a synthesis of the infinite and the finite, of the temporal and the eternal, of freedom and necessity. In short a synthesis. A synthesis is a relation between two terms. Looked at in this way a human being is not yet a self.

In a relation between two things the relation is the third term in the form of a negative unity,[5] and the two relate to the relation, and in the relation to that relation; this is what it is from the point of view of soul for soul and body to be in relation.[6] If, on the other hand, the relation relates to itself, then this relation is the positive third, and this is the self.

Such a relation, which relates to itself, a self, must either have established itself or been established by something else.

If the relation which relates to itself has been established by something else, then of course the relation is the third term, but then this relation, the third term, is a relation which relates in turn to that which has established the whole relation.

Such a derived, established relation is the human self, a relation which relates to itself, and in relating to itself relates to something else. That is why there can be two forms of authentic despair. If the human self were self-established, there would only be a question of one form: not wanting to be itself, wanting to be rid of itself. There could be no question of wanting in despair to be oneself. For this latter formula is the expression of the relation's (the self's) total dependence, the expression of the fact that the self cannot by itself arrive at or remain in equilibrium and rest, but only, in relating to itself, by relating to that which has established the whole relation. Indeed, so far from its being simply the case that this second form of despair (wanting in despair to be oneself) amounts to a special form on its own, all despair can in the end be resolved into or reduced to it. If a person in despair is, as he thinks, aware of his despair and doesn't refer to it mindlessly as something that happens to him (rather in the way someone suffering from vertigo talks through an internally caused delusion about a weight on his head, or its being as though something were pressing down on him, etc., neither the weight nor the pressure being anything external but an inverted image of the internal), and wants now on his own, all on his own, and with all his might to remove the despair, then he is still in despair and through all his seeming effort only works himself all the more deeply into a deeper despair. The imbalance[7] in despair is not a simple imbalance but an imbalance in a relation that relates to itself and which is established by something else. So the lack of balance in that 'for-itself' relationship also reflects itself infinitely in the relation to the power which established it.

This then is the formula which describes the state of the self when despair is completely eradicated: in relating to itself and in wanting to be itself, the self is grounded transparently in the power that established it.

B

The possibility and actuality of despair

Is despair a merit or a defect? Purely dialectically it is both. If one were to think of despair only in the abstract, without reference to some particular despairer, one would have to say it is an enormous merit. The possibility of this sickness is man's advan-

thinking red

tage over the beast, and it is an advantage which characterizes him quite otherwise than the upright posture, for it bespeaks the infinite erectness or loftiness of his being spirit. The possibility of this sickness is man's advantage over the beast; to be aware of this sickness is the Christian's advantage over natural man; to be cured of this sickness is the Christian's blessedness.

Consequently it is an infinite merit to be able to despair. And yet not only is it the greatest misfortune and misery actually to be in despair; no, it is ruin. Generally the relation between possibility and actuality[8] is not like this; if the ability to be such and such is meritorious, then it is an even greater merit actually to be it. That is to say, in relation to being able, being is an ascent. In the case of despair, however, in relation to being able to be, actually being is one of descent. As infinite as is possibility's merit, just so great is the descent. So what amounts to an ascent in the case of despair is *not* being in it. Yet this way of putting it is again ambiguous. Not being in despair is not the same as not being lame, blind, and so on. If not being in despair means neither more nor less than not being in despair, then it is precisely to be in despair. Not being in despair must mean the annihilated possibility of the ability to be in it. For it to be true that someone is not in despair, he must be annihilating that possibility every instant. Usually the relation between possibility and actuality is not like this. For although the thinkers[9] say that actuality is annihilated possibility, that is not entirely true; it is the fulfilled, the active possibility. Here, on the contrary, the actuality (not being in despair), which is thus also a negation, is the possibility annihilated, rendered impotent. Usually the relation of the actual to the possible is one of confirmation; here it is a denial.

Despair is the imbalance in a relation of synthesis, in a relation which relates to itself. But the synthesis is not the imbalance, the synthesis is just the possibility; or, the possibility of the imbalance lies in the synthesis. If the synthesis were itself the imbalance, there would be no despair; it would be something that lay in human nature itself, that is, it would not be despair; it would be something that happened to a person, something he suffered, like a sickness he succumbs to, or like death, which is the fate of everyone. No, despair lies in the person himself. But if he were not a synthesis there would be no question of his despairing; nor could he despair unless the synthesis were originally in the right relationship from the hand of God.

Where then does despair come from? From the relation in which the synthesis relates to itself, from the fact that God, who made man this relation, as it were lets go of it; that is, from the relation's relating to itself. And in the fact that the relation is spirit, is the self, lies the accountability under which all despair is, every moment, what it is, however much and however ingeniously the despairer, deceiving both himself and others, speaks of his despair as a misfortune – through a confusion as in the afore-mentioned case of vertigo, with which despair, though different in kind, has much in common, vertigo being under the aspect of soul what despair is under the aspect of spirit, and pregnant with analogies to despair.

So when the imbalance, despair, occurs, does it continue as a matter of course? No, not as a matter of course. If it continues, that is due not to the imbalance but to the relation which relates to itself. That is to say, every time the imbalance manifests itself, and every moment it exists, one must go back to the relation. Note how one talks of someone bringing a sickness upon himself, through carelessness say. So the sickness sets in and from that moment it takes effect and is now something *actual*, and its origin becomes more and more *past*. It would be both cruel and inhuman to keep on saying, 'You, the patient, are this very moment bringing sickness upon yourself', that is, perpetually to resolve the actuality of the sickness into its possibility. It is true that he brought the disease upon himself, but he did that only once; the perseverance of the sickness is a simple consequence of the fact that that is what he once did; its progress is not to be referred every moment to him as its cause. He brought it upon himself, but one cannot say, 'He *is bringing it upon himself.*' Not so with despair. Every actual moment of despair is to be referred back to its possibility; every moment he despairs he *brings it upon himself*; the time is constantly the present: nothing actual, past and done with, comes about; at every moment of actual despair the despairer bears with him all that has gone before as something present in the form of possibility. This is because despair is an aspect of spirit, it has to do with the eternal in a person. But the eternal is something he cannot be rid of, not in all eternity. He cannot rid himself of it once and for all; nothing is more impossible. Every moment he doesn't have it, he must have cast or be casting it off – but it returns, that is, every moment he despairs he brings the despair upon himself. For despair is not a result of the imbalance, but of the relation which relates to itself. And the relation to himself is something a human being cannot be rid of, just as little as he can be rid of himself, which for that matter is one and the same thing, since the self is indeed the relation to oneself.

subjective which solves
C

Despair is 'the sickness unto death'

We must none the less understand this concept, the sickness unto death, in a special sense. Ordinarily, it would mean a sickness the end and outcome of which is death. Thus one would speak of sickness unto death synonymously with a fatal illness. In this sense despair cannot be called the sickness unto death. But in the Christian understanding death is itself a passing into life. For that matter, in Christian terms, no earthly, physical sickness is unto death. For death is no doubt the end of the sickness, but death is not the end. If, in the strictest sense, there is to be any question of a sickness unto death, it must be one where the end is death and where death is the end. And thinking that is precisely to despair.

Yet despair is the sickness unto death in another and still more definite sense. For there is not the remotest possibility of dying of this sickness in the straightforward sense, or of this sickness ending in physical death. On the contrary, the torment of despair is precisely the inability to die. In this it has much in common with the condition of the mortally ill person who is in the throes of death but cannot die. Thus to be sick unto death is to be unable to die, yet not as though there were hope of life. No, the hopelessness is that even the last hope, death, is gone. When death is the greatest danger, one hopes for life. But when one learns to know the even more horrifying danger, one hopes for death. When the danger is so great that death has become the hope, then despair is the hopelessness of not even being able to die.

It is in this latter sense, then, that despair is the sickness unto death, this tormenting contradiction, this sickness in the self; eternally to die, to die and yet not to die, to die death itself. For to die means that it is all over, while to die death itself means to live to experience dying. And if one can live to experience this for a single moment, then one lives to experience it for ever. If someone is to die of despair as one dies of an illness, then the eternal in him, the self, must be able to die in the same sense that the body dies of the illness. But this is impossible: dying in despair transforms itself constantly into a living. The despairer cannot die; no more than 'the dagger can kill thoughts'[10] can despair consume the eternal, the self that is the source of despair, whose worm dieth not and whose fire is not quenched.[11] Yet despair is exactly a consumption of the *self*, but an impotent self-consumption not capable of doing what it wants. But what it wants is to consume itself, which it cannot do, and this impotence is a new form of self-consumption, but in which despair is once again incapable of doing what it wants, to consume itself. This is a heightening of despair, or the law for the heightening of despair. This is the hot incitement or the cold fire in despair,[12] this incessantly inward gnawing, deeper and deeper in impotent self-consumption. Far from its being any comfort to the despairer that the despair doesn't consume him, on the contrary this comfort is just what torments him; this is the very thing that keeps the sore alive and life in the sore. For what he – not despaired but – despairs over is precisely this: that he cannot consume himself, cannot be rid of himself, cannot become nothing. This is the heightened formula for despair, the rising fever in this sickness of the self.

Someone in despair despairs over *something*. So, for a moment, it seems, but only for a moment. That same instant the true despair shows itself, or despair in its true guise. In despairing over *something* he was really despairing over *himself*, and he wants now to be rid of himself. Thus when the power-crazed person whose motto is 'Caesar or nothing'[13] doesn't become Caesar, he despairs over that. But this indicates something else: that he cannot stand being himself precisely because he failed to become Caesar. So really he is in despair not over not becoming Caesar, but over himself for not having become Caesar. This self which, had it become Caesar, would have been everything he desired – though in another sense just as much in despair – this self is now what he can bear least of all. In a deeper sense what he cannot bear is not that he did not become Caesar; what is unbearable is this self which did not become Caesar; or better still, what he cannot bear is that he cannot be rid of himself. By becoming Caesar he would have despairingly been rid of himself, but now he did not become Caesar, and, despairingly, cannot be rid of himself. He is really in despair either way, for he does not have his self, he is not his self. By becoming Caesar he would still not have become himself, he would have been rid of himself. And by not becoming Caesar he despairs at not being able to be rid of himself. So it is superficial (and I dare say typical of those who never observed a person in despair, not even themselves) to remark of someone in despair, as though it were the penalty of despair, 'He is eating himself up.' For that is just what he despairs of doing, that is just what to his torment he cannot do, since with despair a fire takes hold in something that cannot burn, or cannot be burned up – the self.

Consequently, to despair over something is still not really despair. It is the beginning, or it is as when the physician says of a sickness that it hasn't yet declared itself. Next comes the declared despair, despairing over oneself. A young girl despairs of love, she despairs over losing the loved one, because he died or became unfaithful. This despair is not declared. No, she despairs over herself. This self of hers, which if it had become 'his' beloved, she would have been rid of, or lost, in the most blissful manner – this self, since it is destined to be a self without 'him', is now an embarrassment; this self, which should have been her *richesse* – though in another sense just as much in despair – has become, now that 'he' is dead, a loathsome void, or a despicable reminder of her betrayal. Just try now, just try saying to such a girl, 'You are eating yourself up', and you will hear her reply, 'Oh no! The pain is just that I can't.'

To despair over oneself, in despair to want to be rid of oneself, is the formula for all despair. So that the second form of despair – wanting in despair to be oneself – can be traced back to the first – in despair not wanting to be oneself – rather as in the aforegoing we resolved the form, 'in despair not wanting to be oneself' into 'wanting in despair to be oneself' (cf. *A* [p. 44]). A person in despair wants despairingly to be himself. But surely if he wants despairingly to be himself, he cannot want to be rid of himself. Yes, or so it seems. But closer observation reveals the contradiction to be still the same. The self which, in his despair, he wants to be is a self he is not (indeed, to want to be the self he truly is, is the very opposite of despair); that is, he wants to tear his self away from the power which established it. But despite all his despair, this he is incapable of doing. Despite all his despairing efforts, that power is the stronger, and it compels him to be the self he does not want to be. But then this is still wanting to be rid of himself, rid of the self that he is, in order to be the self he himself has chanced upon. To be 'self' in the way he wants to be it, that would be – even if in another sense just as despairing – everything he desired; but to be forced to be 'self' in a way that he doesn't want to be, that is his torment – not being able to be rid of himself.

Socrates proved the immortality of the soul from the fact that the sickness of the soul (sin) does not consume it as the body's sickness consumes the body.[14] One can similarly prove the eternal in a man from the fact that despair cannot consume his self, that this is precisely the torment of contradiction in despair. If there were nothing eternal in a man, he would simply be unable to despair. But if despair were able to consume his self, then it couldn't really have been despair in the first place.

This then is the manner in which despair, this sickness in the self, is the sickness unto death. The despairer is mortally ill. It is, although in a sense quite different from any physical illness, the most vital parts that the sickness has attacked; and yet he cannot die. Death is not the end of the sickness, but death is incessantly the end. To be saved from this sickness by death is an impossibility, for the sickness and its torment – and death – are precisely to be unable to die.

That is the condition of despair. However much it eludes the despairer, however much (as must be especially the case with the kind of despair which is ignorance of being in despair) the despairer has succeeded in altogether losing his self, and in such a way that the loss is not in the least way noticeable, eternity will nevertheless make it evident that his condition is that of despair, and will nail him to his self so that the torment will still be that he cannot be rid of his self, and it will be evident that his success was an illusion. And this eternity must do, because having a self, being a self, is the greatest, the infinite, concession that has been made to man, but also eternity's claim on him.

We want to annihilate ourselves

No Jm,

B. The Generality of this Sickness (Despair)

Just as a physician might say there isn't a single human being
who enjoys perfect health, so someone with a proper knowledge of man might say there is not a single human being who
does not despair at least a little, in whose innermost being there
does not dwell an uneasiness, an unquiet, a discordance, an
anxiety in the face of an unknown something, or a something
he doesn't even dare strike up acquaintance with, an anxiety
about a possibility in life or an anxiety about himself, so that as a
physician speaks of one's going about with an illness in the
body, he goes about with a sickness, goes about weighed down
with a sickness of the spirit, which only now and then reveals its
presence within, in glimpses, and with what is for him an
inexplicable anxiety. And besides, there is no one and has never
been anyone outside Christendom who isn't in despair; and
no one in Christendom who is not a true Christian; and so far
as he is not wholly that, then he is still to some extent in
despair.

This observation will no doubt strike many as paradoxical, an
exaggeration, and a gloomy and discouraging view besides. Yet
it is none of these things. It is not gloomy; on the contrary it tries
to shed light on what one generally banishes to a certain
obscurity. It is not discouraging; on the contrary it is uplifting,
since it views every man with regard to the highest demand
that can be made of him: to be spirit. Nor is it paradoxical; on the
contrary it is a consistently worked-out basic view and, as far as
that goes, no exaggeration.

The common view of despair, however, goes no further than
the appearances, and it is therefore a superficial view, that is, no
view. It assumes that every man knows best himself whether or
not he is in despair. So that whoever says he is in despair is
assumed to be so, but also whoever thinks he is not is assumed
not to be. As a result, despair becomes a rather rare phenom-
enon, instead of being quite common. What is rare is not that

someone should be in despair; no, what is rare, the great rarity, is that one should truly not be in despair.

But the common view has a very poor understanding of despair. Among other things, it altogether overlooks (just to mention something which, properly grasped, brings thousands upon thousands and millions under the category of despair) – it altogether overlooks that the very fact of not being in despair, of not being conscious of being in despair, is itself a form of despair. One finds in the common view's grasp of despair, in a far deeper sense, what one sometimes finds with its decisions about whether a person is ill or not – in a far deeper sense; for the popular view has far less knowledge of what spirit is than of sickness and health (and without that one cannot have knowledge of despair either). Commonly a person is assumed to be healthy if he himself doesn't say that he is ill; even more so if he says he is well. A physician, on the other hand, looks on the illness differently. And why? Because the physician has a definite and articulate conception of what it is to be healthy, and tests a person's condition against this. The physician knows that just as there can be merely imagined illness, so too is there merely imagined health. For the latter, therefore, he first takes measures that will bring the illness to view. In general, the physician, just because he is a physician (with knowledge and discernment), does not have unconditional faith in a person's own assertions about his state of health. If what every person said about his state of health – whether he is healthy or sick, where the trouble lies, etc. – could be unconditionally trusted, then the role of physician would be mere fantasy. For a physician's task is not just to prescribe medicines, but first and foremost to diagnose the sickness, and so again, first and foremost, to determine whether the supposedly sick person is really ill, or whether the supposedly healthy person is perhaps in fact ill. Similarly with the psychic expert's relation to despair. He knows what despair is, he is familiar with it and so is not satisfied with a person's declaration either that he is in despair or that he is not. For it must be pointed out that there is a sense in which not even those who say they are in despair always are so. One can affect despair, and one can be mistaken and confuse despair, which is a characteristic of spirit, with all sorts of passing dejection or distraction which go over without coming to the point of despair. But sure enough the psychic expert regards these, too, as forms of despair; he sees quite clearly that it is affectation – but precisely that affectation is despair; he sees quite clearly that this depression etc. is of no great significance – but precisely that fact, that it neither has nor acquires any great significance, is despair.

Furthermore, the common view overlooks the fact that, when compared with illness, despair differs dialectically from what one usually calls sickness, because it is a sickness of the spirit. And this dialectical aspect, properly understood, brings further thousands under the category of despair. If at any time a physician is convinced that so and so is in good health, and then later that person becomes ill, then the physician may well be right about his *having been* well at the time but now being sick. Not so with despair. Once despair appears, what is apparent is that the person was in despair. In fact, it's never possible at any time to decide anything about a person who is not saved through having been in despair. For when whatever causes a person to despair occurs, it is immediately evident that he has been in despair his whole life. When someone gets a fever on the other hand, it cannot possibly be said that now it is evident that he has had a fever all his life. But despair is a characteristic of the spirit, is related to the eternal, and therefore has something of the eternal in its dialectic.

Not only does despair differ from an illness in having a different dialectic, but also in the fact that with regard to despair every characteristic is dialectical; and so the superficial view so easily lets you down in deciding whether or not despair is present. Not to be in despair may mean precisely to be in despair, and it may also mean having been saved from being in despair. A sense of security and repose may mean that one is in despair; that very security, that very peace, can be despair.

It may also mean that one has got the better of despair and won peace. Not being in despair is not like not being ill, for, after all, not being ill cannot be being ill, whereas not being in despair may exactly be to be in despair. It is not the case with despair as it is with illness, where the feeling of indisposition is the illness. By no means. Here again, the feeling of indisposition is dialectical. Never to have had a sense of this indisposition is precisely to be in despair.

This means, and stems from the fact, that regarded as spirit (and if there is to be any question of despair, man has to be regarded under the aspect of spirit), the human condition is always critical. We speak of a crisis in connection with illness but not health. And why not? Because physical health is an immediate characteristic which only becomes dialectical in the state of sickness, where there is then talk of the crisis. But spiritually, or when man is regarded as spirit, health and sickness are both critical. There is no immediate state of spiritual health.

As soon as man ceases to be regarded under the aspect of spirit (and unless he is regarded in that way, neither can there be any question of despair), but merely as a synthesis of soul and body, then health becomes an immediate characteristic, and it is only in the soul's or the body's sickness that the dialectical arises. But despair is exactly man's unconsciousness of being characterized as spirit. Even what humanly speaking is the most beautiful and loveliest thing of all – a womanly youthfulness which is sheer peace and harmony and joy – is nevertheless despair. For while it can be counted the greatest good fortune,[15] good fortune is not a specification of spirit, and deep, deep inside, deep within good fortune's most hidden recesses, there dwells also the dread that is despair. It would be only too glad to be allowed to remain in there, for that is where despair has its most cherished, its choicest dwelling-place: deep in the heart of happiness.[16] All immediacy, in spite of its illusory security and peace, is dread; and, quite consistently therefore, it is most in dread of nothing. In immediacy the most terrifying description of the most horrifying and definite something cannot inspire so much dread as a shrewd half-word almost casually let slip but surely and calculatingly aimed by reflection, about something indeterminate. Yes, one inspires immediacy with the greatest dread of all by subtly letting it believe that it knows what one is talking about. For although immediacy surely doesn't know, reflection never traps its prey more surely than when it makes its snare out of nothing, and reflection is never more itself than when it is – nothing. It requires an eminent reflection, or rather a great faith, to sustain a reflection on nothing, which is to say an infinite reflection. So even the most beautiful and lovely thing of all, a womanly youthfulness, is nevertheless despair, is happiness, the greatest good fortune.[17] One will scarcely have the good fortune to slip through life with this immediacy. And should this good fortune have the good fortune to slip through life, yes, it doesn't help much, because it is despair. For just because it is wholly dialectical, despair is that sickness of which it is true that it is the greatest bad fortune never to have had it; it is truly providential to get it, even though it is the most dangerous of all sicknesses if one does not want to be cured of it. Usually it is being cured of a sickness that we speak of in terms of good fortune, the sickness itself is the misfortune.

It is therefore as far as possible from the truth that the common view is right which assumes despair to be something rare; on the contrary it is quite general. It is as far as possible from the truth that the common view is right which assumes that anyone who doesn't think or feel he is in despair is not in despair, and that only the person who says he is in despair is so. On the contrary, he who says without pretence that he despairs is, after all, a little nearer, a dialectical step nearer being cured than all those who are not regarded and who do not regard themselves as being in despair. But, as the connoisseur of souls will no doubt concede, the normal situation is exactly this: that most people live without being properly conscious of being characterized as spirit – and to this one can trace all the so-called security, contentment with life, etc., which is exactly despair.

People who, on the other hand, say they are in despair are as a rule either those who have so much more profound a nature that they are bound to become conscious of themselves as spirit, or those who have been helped by painful experience and difficult decisions to become conscious of themselves as spirit – either one or the other, for very rare indeed is the one who in truth is not in despair.

Ah! so much is spoken about human need and misery; I try to understand it, have even been closely acquainted with not a little of it. So much is spoken about wasting one's life. But the only life wasted is the life of one who so lived it, deceived by life's pleasures or its sorrows, that he never became decisively, eternally, conscious of himself as spirit, as self, or, what is the same, he never became aware – and gained in the deepest sense the impression – that there is a God there and that 'he', himself, his self, exists before this God, which infinite gain is never come by except through despair. Alas! also this misery, that so many live their lives in this way, defrauded of this most blessed of all thoughts; this misery that one occupies oneself, or, in one's relation to the mass of mankind, occupies them, with everything else, and uses them to provide the living energy for the play on life's stage, yet never reminds them of this blessedness; this misery that one heaps them together and defrauds them instead of separating them all from one another so that each individual may gain the highest, the only thing worth living for, and enough to live in for an eternity. Methinks I could weep for an eternity for the fact that this misery exists! Ah! and here to my mind we have one expression more of the horror of this most dreadful of all sicknesses and misery, namely its hiddenness. Not just that someone suffering from it can wish to hide it, and may be able to do so, not just that it can live in a person in such a way that no one, no one at all, discovers it. No, but that it can be so concealed in a person that he himself is not aware of it! Ah! and when the hour-glass has run out, the hour-glass of temporality, when the worldly tumult is silenced and the restless or unavailing urgency comes an end, when all about

Rousseau

Consciousness is
Key – Hegel steps of
this

you is still as it is in eternity – whether you are man or woman, rich or poor, dependent or free, happy or unhappy; whether you bore in your elevation the splendour of the crown or in humble obscurity only the toil and heat of the day; whether your name will be remembered for as long as the world lasts, and so will have been remembered as long as it lasted, or you are without a name and run namelessly with the numberless multitude; whether the glory that surrounded you surpassed all human description, or the severest and most ignominious human judgement was passed on you – eternity asks you, and every one of these millions of millions, just one thing: whether you have lived in despair or not, whether so in despair that you did not know that you were in despair, or in such a way that you bore this sickness concealed deep inside you as your gnawing secret, under your heart like the fruit of a sinful love, or in such a way that, a terror to others, you raged in despair. If then, if you have lived in despair, then whatever else you won or lost, for you everything is lost, eternity does not acknowledge you, it never knew you, or, still more dreadful, it knows you as you are known, it manacles you to your self in despair!

C. The Forms of this Sickness (Despair)

It must be possible to find out the forms of despair by reflecting on the factors which constitute the self as a synthesis. The self is made up of infinitude and finitude. But this synthesis is a relation, and a relation which, though derived, relates to itself, which is freedom. The self is freedom. But freedom is the dialectical element in the categories of possibility and necessity.

In the main, however, despair must be considered under the aspect of consciousness; it is whether or not despair is conscious that qualitatively distinguishes one form of despair from another. Granted, when raised to the level of a concept all despair is conscious, but it does not follow that the person who is in despair, the one who according to the concept may be said to despair, is himself conscious of it. Thus consciousness is the decisive factor. In general, what is decisive with regard to the self is consciousness, that is to say, self-consciousness. The more consciousness, the more will; the more will, the more self. Someone who has no will at all is no self. But the more will he has, the more self-consciousness he has too.

A

Despair considered without regard to its being conscious or not, and so with regard only to the factors of the synthesis

(a) Despair under the aspect of finitude / infinitude

The self is the conscious synthesis of infinitude and finitude, which relates to itself, whose task is to become itself, which can only be done in the relationship to God. To become oneself, however, is to become something concrete. But to become something concrete is neither to become finite nor to become infinite, for that which is to become concrete is indeed a synthesis. The development must accordingly consist in infinitely coming away from oneself, in an infinitizing of the self, and in infinitely coming back to oneself in the finitization. If, on the other hand, the self does not become itself, then it is in despair, whether it knows it or not. Yet a self, every moment it exists, is in a process of becoming; for the self κατὰ δύναμιν [kata dynamin – potentially] is not present actually, it is merely what is to come into existence. In so far, then, as the self does not become itself, it is not itself; but not to be oneself is exactly despair.

α. Infinitude's despair is to lack finitude

This follows from the dialectic in the fact that the self is a synthesis, and for this reason either factor is always its opposite. No form of despair can be defined directly (that is, undialectically), but only with reference to its opposite. One can describe the despairer's mental state directly, as indeed writers do by putting the appropriate words into his mouth. But the despair can only be defined by way of its opposite, and if the words are to have any literary value, there must be some reflection of their dialectical opposite in the colouring of their expression. Consequently, every human existence which has supposedly become, or simply wants to be, infinite – yes, any instant in which a human existence has become or simply wants to be infinite – is despair. For the self is a synthesis in which the finite is the confining factor, the infinite the expanding factor. Infinitude's despair is therefore the fantastic, the boundless; for the self is only healthy and free from despair when, precisely by having despaired, it is grounded transparently in God.

The fantastic is, of course, most closely related to the imagination [Phantasien], but the imagination is related in its turn to feeling, understanding, and will, so that a person's feelings, understanding and will may be fantastic. Fantasy is, in general, the medium of infinitization. It is not a faculty like the other faculties – if one wishes to speak in this way, it is the faculty instar omnium [for all faculties]. What feelings, understanding and will a person has depends in the last resort upon what

we don't want the synthesis

imagination he has – how he represents himself to himself,[18] that is, upon imagination. Imagination is the infinitizing reflection, which is why the elder Fichte quite correctly assumed that the imagination is the source of the categories even with regard to knowledge.[19] The self is reflection and the imagination is reflection, the self's representation of itself in the form of the self's possibility. The imagination is the whole of reflection's possibility; and the intensity of this medium is the possibility of the self's intensity.

The fantastic is generally speaking what carries a person into the infinite in such a way that it only leads him away from himself and thus prevents him from coming back to himself.

When emotion becomes fantastic in this way, the self is simply more and more volatilized and eventually becomes a kind of abstract sensitivity which inhumanly belongs to no human, but which inhumanly participates sensitively, so to speak, in the fate of some abstraction, for example, humanity *in abstracto*. Just as the rheumatic isn't master of his physical sensations, which are so subject to wind and weather that he cannot help registering changes in the air, etc., so it is with the person whose emotions have become fantastic. In a way he becomes infinitized, but not in such a way as to become more and more himself, for he loses himself more and more.

Similarly when understanding becomes fantastic. The law for the development of the self in respect of understanding, so long as it remains true that the self is becoming itself, is that every increase in understanding corresponds to a greater degree of self-understanding, that the more it knows, the more it knows itself. When this does not happen, the more understanding increases, the more it becomes a kind of inhuman knowledge in the production of which man's self is squandered, much as men were squandered in the building of the pyramids, or as men were squandered in Russian brass bands on playing just one note, neither more nor less.[20]

When the will becomes fantastic, the self is similarly increasingly volatilized. The will then does not become as consistently concrete as it becomes abstract, so that the more it is infinitized in its purpose and decision, the closer and more contemporaneous it becomes with itself in that small part of the task which can be carried out now, immediately, so that in being infinitized it comes back to itself in the strictest sense, so that when *furthest away* from itself (when it is most infinitized in its purpose and decision), it is simultaneously *as near as can be* to itself in the carrying out of the infinitely small part of the task that can be accomplished this very day, this very hour, this very moment.

And when feeling or understanding or will has become fantastic, then in the end the whole self can become that, whether in a more active form, where the person plunges headlong into the fantastic, or in a more passive form and he is carried off into it, though he is responsible in both cases. The self then leads a fantastic existence in abstract infinitization or in abstract isolation, constantly lacking its self, from which it simply gets further and further away. Take the religious sphere, for example. The relationship to God is an infinitizing, but here a person may be so carried away that the infinitizing becomes simply an intoxication. Existing before God may seem unendurable to someone, because it is impossible for him to come back to himself, become himself. A fantastic religious individual of this kind would say (to present him with the help of some lines): 'That a sparrow can live is comprehensible; it doesn't know it exists before God. But to know that one exists before God and not that very instant go mad or become nothing!'

But to become fantastic in this way, and therefore be in despair, although usually obvious, does not mean that a person may not continue living a fairly good life, to all appearances be someone, employed with temporal matters, get married, beget children, be honoured and esteemed – and one may fail to notice that in a deeper sense he lacks a self. Such things cause little stir in the world; for in the world a self is what one least asks after, and the thing it is most dangerous of all to show signs of having. The biggest danger, that of losing oneself, can pass off in the world as quietly as if it were nothing; every other loss, an arm, a leg, five dollars, a wife, etc. is bound to be noticed.

β. Finitude's despair is to lack infinitude

This follows, as shown under (α) [p. 60], from the dialectic in the fact that the self is a synthesis, and for this reason either factor is its opposite.

To lack infinitude is despairing confinement, narrowness. It is, of course, a question here only of ethical narrowness and limitation. The world really only interests itself in intellectual or aesthetic limitations, or in the indifferent, which is always what the world talks about most. For worldliness is precisely to ascribe infinite value to the indifferent. The worldly point of view always clings closely to the difference between man and man, and has naturally no understanding (since to have it is spirituality) of the one thing needful,[21] and therefore no understanding of that limitation and narrowness which is to have lost oneself, not by being volatilized in the infinite, but by being altogether finitized, by instead of being a self, having become a cipher, one more person, one more repetition of this perpetual *Einerlei* [one-and-the-same].

Despairing narrow-mindedness is to lack primitiveness, or to have stripped oneself of one's primitiveness, from a spiritual point of view to have emasculated oneself. For every human being is primitively organized as a self, characteristically determined to become himself; and although indeed every such self has sharp edges, that means only that it is to be worked smooth, not ground away, not through fear of man wholly abandon being itself, or even through fear of man simply not dare to be itself in that more essential contingency (which precisely is not to be ground away) in which a person is still himself for himself. But while one kind of despair steers blindly in the infinite and loses itself, another kind of despair allows itself to be, so to speak, cheated of its self by 'the others'. By seeing the multitude of people around it, by being busied with all sorts of worldly affairs, by being wise to the ways of the world, such a person

63

forgets himself, in a divine sense forgets his own name, dares not believe in himself, finds being himself too risky, finds it much easier and safer to be like the others, to become a copy, a number, along with the crowd.

Now this form of despair goes practically unnoticed in the world. Precisely by losing himself in this way, such a person gains all that is required for a flawless performance in everyday life, yes, for making a great success out of life. Here there is no dragging of the feet, no difficulty with his self and its infinitizing, he is ground as smooth as a pebble, as exchangeable as a coin of the realm. Far from anyone thinking him to be in despair, he is just what a human being ought to be. Naturally the world has generally no understanding of what is truly horrifying. The despair that not only does not cause any inconvenience in life, but makes life convenient and comfortable, is naturally enough in no way regarded as despair. That this is the worldly view is evident, among other things, from nearly all the proverbs, which are nothing but rules of prudence. For example, it is said that one rues ten times having spoken, for the one time one rues one's silence. And why? Because the external fact of having spoken can involve one in disagreeable consequences, since it is something actual. But to have kept silent! Yet this is the most dangerous of all. For in staying silent a person is thrown wholly upon his own devices: here actuality does not come to his aid by punishing him, by heaping on him the consequences of his words. No, in this respect it is easy enough to keep silent. But for that very reason the person who knows the true object of dread fears more than anything any fault, any sin, that takes an inward turn and leaves no trace in the outside world. The world thinks it is dangerous to venture in this way, and why? Because one might lose; the prudent thing is not to venture. And yet by not venturing it is so dreadfully easy to lose what would be hard to lose by venturing and which, whatever you lost, you will in any case never lose in this way, so easily, so completely, as though it were nothing – oneself. For if I have ventured wrongly, very well, life then helps me with its penalty. But if I haven't ventured at all, who helps me then? And when, into the bargain, by not venturing at all in the highest sense (and to venture in the highest sense is precisely to become aware of oneself) I cravenly gain all earthly advantages – and lose myself! . . .

And finitude's despair is just so. A man in this kind of despair can very well live on in temporality; indeed he can do so all the more easily, be to all appearances a human being, praised by others, honoured and esteemed, occupied with all the goals of temporal life. Yes, what we call worldliness simply consists of such people who, if one may so express it, pawn themselves to the world.[22] They use their abilities, amass wealth, carry out worldly enterprises, make prudent calculations, etc., and perhaps are mentioned in history, but they are not themselves. In a spiritual sense they have no self, no self for whose sake they could venture everything, no self for God – however selfish they are otherwise.

(b) Despair viewed under the aspect of possibility / necessity

For the purposes of becoming (and the self must become itself freely) possibility and necessity are equally essential. Just as infinitude and finitude (ἄπειρον-πέρᾰς) [apeiron-peras] belong to the self,[23] so also do possibility and necessity. A self that has no possibility is in despair, and likewise a self that has no necessity.

α. Possibility's despair is to lack necessity
This, as was shown, follows from the dialectic.

Just as finitude is the confining factor in relation to infinitude, so necessity is the constraining factor in relation to possibility. In so far as the self as a synthesis of finitude and infinitude is established, and so exists κατὰ δύναμιν [kata dynamin – potentially] now to become [itself], it is reflected in the medium of imagination, and that means the infinite possibility comes into view. Κατὰ δύναμιν the self is just as much possible as necessary; although it is indeed itself, it has to become itself. To the extent that it is itself, it is necessary; and to the extent that it must become itself, it is a possibility.

Now if possibility outstrips necessity, the self runs away from itself in possibility so that it has no necessity to return to. This then is possibility's despair. Here the self becomes an abstract possibility; it exhausts itself floundering about in possibility, yet it never moves from where it is nor gets anywhere, for necessity is just that 'where'. Becoming oneself is a movement one makes just where one is. Becoming is a movement *from* some place, but becoming oneself is a movement *at* that place.

Thus possibility seems greater and greater to the self; more and more becomes possible because nothing becomes actual. In the end it seems as though everything were possible, but that is the very moment that the self is swallowed up in the abyss. Even a small possibility needs some time to become actual. But eventually the time that should be spent on actuality gets shorter and shorter, everything becomes more and more momentary. Although possibility becomes more and more intensive, it is in possibility's sense, not actuality's; for in actuality's sense what is intensive is that at least something of what is possible becomes actual. Just when one thing seems possible some new possibility arises, and finally these phantasms succeed one another with such speed that it seems as though everything were possible, and that is the very moment the individual himself has finally become nothing but an atmospheric illusion.

Surely what the self now lacks is actuality; that at least is what would normally be said, and indeed we imply this when we talk of a person's having become unreal. But on closer examination what the self really lacks is necessity. For it is not the case, as the philosophers would explain it, that necessity is a unity of possibility and actuality;[24] no, actuality is the unity of possibility and necessity. Nor is it merely lack of strength that makes a self lose itself in possibility, at least not as usually understood. What is really missing is the strength to obey, to yield to the necessary in one's self, what might be called one's limits. Nor therefore is it the misfortune of such a self not to have become anything in the world; no, the misfortune is that he did not become aware of himself, that the self he is is a quite definite something, and thus the necessary. Instead, through this self's fantastically reflecting itself in possibility, he lost himself. Even to see one*self* in a mirror one must recognize oneself, for unless one does that, one does not see one*self*, only a human being. But the mirror of possibility is no ordinary mirror; it must be used with the utmost caution. For in this case the mirror is, in the highest sense, a false one. The fact that in the possibility of itself a self appears in such and such a guise is only a half-truth; for in the possibility of itself the self is still far from, or only half of, itself. So the question is what further specification is provided by this self's necessity. Possibility is like offering a child some treat: the child straightaway says yes, but then there's the question of whether the parents will give their consent – and as it is with parents, so it is with necessity.

Yet *everything* is possible in possibility. One can therefore run astray in all possible ways, but essentially in two. The one form is the wishful, the hankering; the other is the melancholic-fantastic (hope in the one case, fear or dread in the other). Fairy-tales and legends often tell of a knight who suddenly catches sight of a rare bird of which he then sets off in pursuit, since in the beginning it seemed quite close, but then it flies off again, until at last night falls. The knight is separated from his companions and lost in the wilderness in which he now finds himself. Similarly with wish's possibility. Instead of taking possibility back to necessity he runs after possibility – and in the end cannot find the way back to himself. Much the same happens in melancholy but in the opposite direction. The individual pursues with melancholic love one of dread's possibilities, which in the end takes him away from himself, so he perishes in the dread, or perishes in what it was he was in dread of perishing in.

β. Necessity's despair is to lack possibility

If one wants to compare running astray in possibility with a child's use of vowels, then lacking possibility is like being dumb. The necessary is as though there were only consonants, but to utter them there has to be possibility. If that is lacking, when a human existence is brought to the point where it lacks possibility, it is in despair and is so every moment it lacks possibility.

There is commonly thought to be a certain age at which people are especially rich in hope, or people talk of there being or having been a certain period in their lives or a particular moment when they were so rich in hope and possibility. But all that is just a human manner of speech which does not get to the truth; all that hope and all that despair is not yet the true hope nor the true despair.

The decisive thing is: for God everything is possible. This is eternally true and therefore true every moment. People no doubt say this in the ordinary way of things, and this is how one ordinarily puts it, but the decisive moment only comes when man is brought to the utmost extremity, where in human terms there is no possibility. Then the question is whether he will believe that for God everything is possible, that is, whether he will *have faith*. But this is simply the formula for losing one's mind; to have faith is precisely to lose one's mind so as to win God. Let us suppose it goes as follows. A person, shuddering in the grip of a terrified imagination, imagines some horror which for him would be absolutely unendurable. Then it happens, this very horror happens to him. In human terms nothing could be more certain than his undoing – and the despair in his soul fights desperately to be allowed to despair, for the peace of mind, if you will, in which to despair, for the consent of his whole being to and in the despair, so that he would curse nothing or nobody more than the attempt, or the one who took a hand, at preventing him from despairing. As the poets' poet superbly, incomparably expresses it (*Richard II*, Act 3, Scene 2):[25]

> Beshrew thee, cousin, which didst lead me forth
> Of that sweet way I was in to despair.

Salvation, then, is humanly speaking the most impossible thing of all; but for God everything is possible! This is the struggle of *faith*, which struggles insanely, if you will, for possibility. For only possibility saves. When someone faints, people shout for water, Eau-de-Cologne, Hoffman's drops. But for someone who is on the point of despair it is: get me possibility, get me possibility, the only thing that can save me is possibility! A possibility and the despairer breathes again, he revives; for without possibility it is as though a person cannot draw breath. Sometimes the inventiveness of human imagination is all one needs to come by possibility, but in the end, that is, when the question is one of having *faith*, the only thing that helps is that for God everything is possible.

So goes the struggle. Whether the person who thus contends goes under depends entirely on whether he gets hold of a possibility, that is to say, on whether he will *have faith*. And yet, he understands that humanly speaking nothing could be more certain than his undoing. This is what is dialectical in having faith. In general all a person knows is that this and that, as he hopes and expects, etc., is not going to happen to him. If it does, he goes under. The foolhardy person throws himself deliberately into danger, where the possibility may also be this and that; and if it happens, he despairs and goes under. The *believer* sees and understands his undoing (in what has befallen him or what he risks) in human terms, but he has faith. Therefore he does not go under. The manner in which he is to be helped he leaves wholly to God, but he believes that for God everything is possible. To *believe* in his own undoing is impossible. To grasp that humanly it is his undoing and yet believe in possibility is to have faith.[26] Then, too, God helps him, perhaps by letting him avoid the horror, perhaps through the horror itself; that help unexpectedly, miraculously, divinely, turns up. Miraculously, for it is a remarkable piece of pedantry to suppose that a person's being miraculously helped could only have happened eighteen hundred years ago. Whether a person has been miraculously helped essentially depends on with what passion of mind he has grasped that help was impossible, and in the next instance on how honest he is towards the power which nevertheless helped him. But people as a rule do neither the one nor the other; they shriek that help is impossible without ever taxing their minds on how to find help, and afterwards they ungratefully lie.

The believer possesses the ever-sure antidote to despair: possibility; since for God everything is possible at every moment. This is the health of faith which resolves contradictions. The contradiction here is that in human terms the undoing is certain and that still there is possibility. Health is in general to be able to resolve contradictions. Thus bodily or physically: a draught of air is a contradiction, for a current of air is cold and warm disparately or undialectically; but a healthy body resolves this contradiction and does not notice the draught. So too with faith.

To lack possibility means either that everything has become necessary or that everything has become trivial.

The determinist, the fatalist, is in despair, and in despair he has lost his self because for him everything is necessity. He is like that king who starved to death because all his food turned to gold.[27] Personhood is a synthesis of possibility and necessity. Its manner of being is therefore like breathing (respiration),[28] which is aspiration and expiration. The determinist's self cannot breathe because it is impossible to breathe necessity alone, which on its own suffocates the human self. The fatalist is in despair, he has lost God and thereby his self; for a person who has no God has no self either. But the fatalist has no God, or, what is the same, his God is necessity. Since for God everything is possible, then God is that everything is possible. The fatalist's worship of God is therefore at most an interjection, and really it is muteness, mute submission, he is unable to pray. To pray is also to breathe, and possibility is for the self what oxygen is for breathing. But it is no more possible for either possibility or necessity alone to provide the conditions for the breath of prayer than for a person to breathe only oxygen or nitrogen. In order to pray there has to be a God, a self – and possibility, or a self and possibility in the cogent sense, for God is the fact that everything is possible, or that everything is possible is God. And only the person whose being was so shaken that he became spirit by grasping that everything is possible, only he has had dealings with God. The fact that God's will is the possible means I can pray; if God's will is only the necessary, then man is essentially as dumb as the beast.

But with petty bourgeois vulgarity and triviality, which also essentially lack possibility, the case is somewhat different. The petty bourgeois is spiritless, while the determinist and the fatalist are in a state of spiritual despair. But spiritlessness, too, is despair. The petty bourgeois lacks any spiritual characteristic and is absorbed in the probable, in which the possible finds its tiny place. Thus he lacks possibility in the way needed to become aware of God. Devoid of imagination, as the petty bourgeois always is, he lives within a certain orbit of trivial experience as to how things come about, what is possible, what usually happens, no matter whether he is a tapster or a prime minister. This is the way in which the petty bourgeois has lost himself and God. For to be aware of his self and of God, a man's imagination must whirl him up higher than the dank air of the probable, it must tear him out of that and, by making possible what exceeds the *quantum satis* [measure of sufficiency] of all experience, teach him to hope and fear, or fear and hope. But imagination is what the petty bourgeois mentality does not have, will not have, shrinks from with horror. So here there is no help. And if life helps now and then with terrors that transcend the parrot-wisdom of banal experience, then the petty bourgeois mentality despairs, that is, it becomes evident that despair is what it was; it lacks faith's possibility in the way needed to be able with God to save a self from certain ruin.

Fatalism and determinism have, after all, imagination

enough to despair of possibility, possibility enough to discover the impossibility. Petty bourgeois vulgarity placates itself in the commonplace, in despair as much when things go well as when they go badly. Fatalism and determinism lack the possibility needed for relaxing and assuaging, for tempering necessity; they lack, that is to say, possibility as mitigation. Petty bourgeois vulgarity lacks possibility as an awakener from spiritlessness. For the petty bourgeois thinks he is in control of possibility, has lured this tremendous elasticity into the snare, or madhouse, of probabilities, thinks he holds it prisoner. He carries possibility about captive in the cage of probability, shows it off, fancies himself to be the master, does not see that in the very act of doing so he has made himself captive as a slave to spiritlessness and is the meanest of all. The person who gets lost in possibility soars with the boldness of despair; but the person for whom all has become necessary strains his back on life, bent down with the weight of despair; but the petty bourgeois mentality spirit-lessly triumphs.

B

Despair viewed under the aspect of consciousness

It is the rising level of consciousness, or the degree to which it rises, that is the continual intensification of despair: the more consciousness the more intense the despair. One sees this everywhere, most clearly in the maximum and minimum of despair. The devil's despair is the most intense despair, for the devil is pure spirit and to that extent absolute consciousness and transparency: in the devil there is no obscurity which might serve as a mitigating excuse; his despair is therefore the most absolute defiance. This is despair at its maximum. At its mini-mum, despair is, yes, as in human terms one might be tempted to put it, a state which in a kind of innocence does not even know that it is despair. So there is least despair when this unconsciousness is at its maximum. Indeed one might almost call it a dialectical question whether such a state can properly be called despair.

(a) The despair which is ignorant of being despair, or the despairing ignorance of having a self and an eternal self

That none the less this condition is indeed despair, and is properly so named, expresses what one might in the best sense call truth's self-righteousness. *Veritas est index sui et falsi.* [Truth is the criterion of itself and of the false.][29] Certainly this self-righteousness is not highly regarded. It is regarded as little as people in general regard the relationship to truth, the relating of oneself to the true, as the highest good, and even less see it Socratically as the greatest misfortune to be in error – their sensuous reactions usually far outweigh their intellect. A person supposedly fortunate in this way, who imagines himself blessed by good fortune but when considered in the light of truth is unfortunate, is usually very far from wanting to be snatched out of this error. On the contrary, he grows indignant, looks on the person who does this as his worst enemy, considers it an assault, something bordering on murder, as one talks of a kill-joy. And the reason? He is totally dominated by his sensuous and psycho-sensuous reactions; he lives in the categories of the sensate, the pleasant and the unpleasant, poo-poos spirit, the truth, etc.; he is too sensate to have the courage to risk and endure being spirit. However vain and conceited people may be, the conception they usually have of themselves is very humble; that is, they have no conception of being spirit, the absolute that a human can be;[30] but vain and conceited they remain – comparatively speaking. If one were to imagine a house consisting of basement, ground floor and first floor, tenanted or planned in such a way that there is, or is meant to be, a difference of social class between the occupants of each floor – and if now one were to compare being a human being with such a house, then the sorry and ludicrous fact with most people is, alas, that in their own house they prefer to live in the

73

basement. Every human being is the psycho-physical synthesis planned as spirit; this is the building, but he prefers living in the basement, that is, in the categories of sensation. Moreover, he not only prefers living in the basement – no, he loves it so much that he is indignant if anyone suggests he occupy the fine suite lying vacant for him; after all he *is* living in his own house!

No, being in error is, quite un-Socratically, what people are least afraid of. One sees amazing examples of this which illustrate it on a stupendous scale. A thinker erects a huge building, a system,[31] one that encompasses the whole of life and world-history, etc. – and if one then turns attention to his personal life one discovers to one's astonishment the appalling and ludicrous fact that he himself does not live in this huge, high-vaulted palace, but in a store-house next door, or a kennel, or at most in the janitor's quarters. If one took it upon oneself to draw attention with but a single word to this contradiction, he would be insulted. For so long as he can complete the system – with the help of his error – being in error is not what he is afraid of.

So the fact that the despairer is ignorant of his state as being one of despair is nothing to the point, he is in despair just the same. If despair [*Fortvivlelse*] is distraction [*Forvildelse*], then not knowing about it simply means he is under a delusion [*Vildfarelse*] as well. The relation between ignorance and despair is like that of ignorance to dread (cf. *The Concept of Dread* by Vigilius Haufniensis);[32] the dread in a spiritless person is recognizable precisely in his spiritless sense of security. Beneath it lies dread all the same, and also beneath it lies despair, and when the spell of the illusion is broken, when life begins to quake, then it is immediately apparent that despair was what was lying beneath.

Compared with the person who is conscious of his despair, the despairer who does not know he is in despair is simply one negativity further from the truth and deliverance.[33] Despair is itself a negativity, ignorance of it a new negativity. But to arrive at the truth one has to pass through every negativity; it is just as the old story says about breaking a certain magic spell: it won't be broken unless the piece is played right through backwards.[34]

However, it is only in one sense – a purely dialectical sense – that the person ignorant of his despair is further from the truth, and from what will deliver him, than the person who knows it yet remains in despair. For in another sense, ethico-dialectically, it is the person who remains in despair and is conscious of his despair who is further from deliverance, because his despair is more intense. Yet ignorance is so far from expunging the despair, or turning it into non-despair, that on the contrary it can be the most dangerous form of despair. In his ignorance the despairer is, though in a way to his own undoing, made safe against becoming aware – which means he is safely in the hands of despair.

In his ignorance of his own despair a person is furthest from being conscious of himself as spirit. But precisely this – not being conscious of oneself as spirit – is despair, that is to say, spiritlessness – whether the state is one of total extinction, a merely vegetative life, or a life full of energy the secret of which is nevertheless despair. In the latter case the despairer is in the same situation as the consumptive: he feels best, considers himself at his healthiest, can appear to others to be in the pink of condition, just when the illness is at its most critical.

This form of despair (ignorance of it) is the most common in the world, yes, what one calls the world, or, more accurately, what Christianity calls the world, paganism and the natural man in Christendom.[35] Paganism as it was historically and is now, and paganism in Christendom, is precisely that kind of despair; it is despair but has no knowledge of it. True, both paganism and natural man make a distinction between being in despair and not being in despair, that is, they talk of despair as though only certain individuals despaired. But this distinction is as unreliable as that which paganism and natural man make between love and self-love, as though all this love were not really self-love.[36] Yet paganism and natural man could not and cannot advance beyond this unreliable distinction, for what characterizes despair is just this – that it is ignorant of being despair.

One easily sees from all this that the aesthetic concept of spiritlessness in no way provides the criterion for judging what is despair and what is not; which for that matter is quite as it should be, since it is impossible to specify aesthetically what spirit truly is. How could you expect the aesthetic individual to answer a question which for him simply does not exist! It would also be excessively stupid to deny that individual pagans, as well as pagan nations *en masse*, have accomplished amazing feats from which writers have drawn and will continue to draw inspiration, or that paganism boasts examples of what cannot be sufficiently admired aesthetically. And it would be foolish, too, to deny that lives are led in paganism which are rich in the greatest aesthetic enjoyment, and that natural man can lead such a life, exploiting in the most tasteful manner every favour granted, even letting art and science serve to heighten, embellish and refine the pleasure. No, the aesthetic point of view with its absence of spirit does not provide the criterion of what is despair and what is not, the point of view which must be adopted is that of the ethico-religious: spirit, or, negatively, lack of spirit, spiritlessness. Every human existence not conscious of itself as spirit, or not personally conscious of itself before God as spirit, every human existence which is not grounded transparently in God, but opaquely rests or merges in some abstract universal (state, nation, etc.), or in the dark about its self, simply takes its capacities to be natural powers, unconscious in a deeper sense of where it has them from, takes its self to be an unaccountable something; if there were any question of accounting for its inner being, every such existence, however astounding its accomplishment, however much it can account for even the whole of existence, however intense its aesthetic enjoyment: every such life is none the less despair. That is what the old Church Fathers meant when they spoke of pagan virtues as splendid vices.[37] They meant that the heart of paganism was despair, that the pagan was not conscious of himself before God as spirit. That is also why the pagan (I offer this as an example but it also has a deeper significance for this whole investigation)

76

had such a remarkably casual attitude to suicide, yes even praised it, something that for spirit is the most critical sin, to flee from existence in this way in rebellion against God. The pagan lacked the spirit's definition of a self, and that is why he judged *sui*-cide in such a way.[38] And this is the same pagan who was particularly severe when it came to theft, fornication, etc. He lacked the perspective for suicide, he lacked the God-relationship and the self. Suicide is inconsequential in purely pagan terms, something anyone can do if he pleases since it is nobody else's business. If suicide were to be cautioned against from the pagan point of view, it would have to be in a long roundabout way that showed how it involved a breach of one's duties to others. The point about suicide, that it is a crime against God himself, altogether escapes the pagan. Therefore, one cannot say that suicide was despair, for that would be a thoughtless hysteron-proteron;[39] one has to say that the fact that the pagan judged suicide in that way was despair.

Nevertheless there is and remains a difference, and it is a difference in kind between paganism in the stricter sense and paganism in Christendom – that difference which Vigilius Haufniensis has drawn attention to in regard to dread, and which is that although paganism lacks spirit, it is pointed in the direction of spirit, while paganism in Christendom lacks spirit in the opposite direction, away from it or in a defection, and is therefore in the strictest sense spiritlessness.

(b) The despair which is conscious of being despair, which is
therefore conscious of having a self in which there is,
however, something eternal, and which now either in
despair does not want to be itself or in despair wants to be
itself

Here, of course, one must distinguish whether the person who is conscious of his despair has the true conception of what despair is. Thus, according to his own conception, he may be right in saying that he is in despair, and yet that is not to say, so far, that he grasps what despair truly is; it may be that if he were to contemplate his life in the light of this concept, he would have to say: 'You are really in even far greater despair than you realize, your despair goes much deeper.' Thus (to recall the above) with the pagan; in regarding himself in comparison with other pagans as being in despair, he was no doubt right about being in despair, but not right about the others not being so; that is, he did not have the true conception of despair.

So conscious despair requires, on the one hand, the true conception of what despair is. On the other, it requires clarity about oneself, or as far as clarity and despair can be conceived together. How far being completely clear about oneself – about the fact that one is in despair – is compatible with actually being in despair, that is to say, whether the clarity of this knowledge and of self-knowledge cannot help but lift a person out of the despair, make him so appalled at himself that he ceases to be in despair, is not a question we will settle here. We won't even try, since this whole matter is one we shall find room for later. Here, however, without pursuing the idea to this dialectical extreme, we merely observe that just as there can be very great variation in the level of consciousness of what despair is, so too with the level of one's consciousness of one's own state as being one of despair. Actual life is too complex to turn up contrasts as abstract as that between a despair that is completely ignorant of being despair and one that is completely conscious of being so. One must assume that in most cases the state of the despairer is one of having only a dim idea, though again with countless nuances, of what that state is. He no doubt realizes in himself to some extent that he is in despair; he is able to detect it in himself as one detects a sickness one goes about with in one's body, but he won't readily admit what the sickness is. At one moment he is almost clear that he is in despair, but then at another it is as though his indisposition had some other cause, something outside him, and if only that were changed he would no longer be in despair. Or perhaps he tries to keep his own condition in the dark by diversions and other means, for example, work and pressure of business, as ways of distracting attention, though again in such a way that he is not altogether clear that he is doing it to keep himself in the dark. Or perhaps he even realizes he is doing this in order to immerse the soul in darkness, does it with a certain perspicacity and shrewd calculation, with psychological insight, but in a deeper sense does not fully realize what he is doing, how despairing his behaviour actually is, etc. For in fact there is in all obscurity and ignorance a dialectical interplay of knowledge and will, and one may make mistakes in trying to understand a person if one stresses only knowledge or only will.

But, as remarked earlier, the level of consciousness intensifies despair. The truer a person's conception of despair, while still remaining in despair, and the more clearly conscious he is of being in despair, the more intense the despair. The person who commits suicide in the consciousness that suicide is despair, and thus far with the true conception of what despair is, is in a more heightened state of despair than someone who commits suicide without the true conception that suicide is despair, while to the contrary the latter's false conception of suicide is the less intense despair. On the other hand, the more clearly conscious the person who commits suicide is of himself (self-consciousness), the more intense is his despair compared with that of someone whose soul is, compared to his, in a state of darkness and confusion.

In the following I shall now examine the two forms of conscious despair in such a way as also to demonstrate a raising of the level of consciousness of what despair is, and of the consciousness that one's condition is one of despair, or what is the same and also the crux, a raising of the level of consciousness of the self. But the opposite to being in despair is to have faith. And so what was earlier proposed as the formula for describing a state in which no despair exists at all, is quite correct, for it is also the formula for faith: in relating to itself and in wanting to be itself, the self is grounded transparently in the power that established it. (Cf. *A*) [p. 44].

α. In despair not wanting to be oneself. The despair of
weakness

Calling this form the despair of weakness already carries some
implication of the second form, (β) [p. 98], wanting in despair
to be oneself. So the opposition is only relative; no despair is
entirely without defiance, indeed defiance is implicit in the very
formulation: *not* wanting to be; while, on the other hand, some
weakness is to be found even in despair's most extreme
defiance. The difference is therefore only relative. The one form
is, so to speak, feminine despair, the other masculine.*

(1) Despair over the earthly or over something earthly

This is pure immediacy, or immediacy with some quantitative
reflection. Here there is no infinite consciousness of the self, of

* Observation of actual life will afford occasional confirmation of the soundness
and hence ultimate correctness of this distinction, and show that it embraces
the whole actuality of despair. For in connection with the child one talks not
of despair but of bad temper, because one is only entitled to assume that the
eternal is present κατὰ δύναμιν [*kata dynamin*] in the child, and not justified
in requiring it of the child as one does of the adult, in whose case it should
actually be present. However, I am far from denying that women may have
forms of masculine despair, and conversely, men feminine forms – but these
are exceptions. Of course the ideal too is rare; it is only in a purely ideal sense
that the distinction between feminine and masculine despair holds absolutely. The woman, however much more tender and sensitive she may be
than the man, has neither the man's egotistically developed conception of the
self, nor in the crucial sense his intellectuality. Her nature is, on the contrary,
to be devoted and selfless, and if it is not that, she is not feminine. Strangely,
no one can be so much a prude (a word that has indeed been coined for
women), so almost cruelly hard to please, as a woman – and yet her nature is
devotedness, and (what is the wonder of it) all this is really a way of
expressing her natural devotedness. For precisely because she bears in her
being all the devotedness of the woman, nature has lovingly provided her
with an instinct, in comparison with which the subtlety of the best-
developed, the most superior reflection of the male is as nothing. This
devotedness of the woman, this, to speak as the Greeks, divine gift and
treasure, is too great a thing to be tossed away blindly. And yet no human
reflection with its sight intact has the keenness of vision to make proper use of
it. For this reason nature has taken care of her: in her blindness she
instinctively sees more clearly than the most clear-sighted reflection; she
instinctively sees what it is she should admire, what it is she should devote
herself to. Devotedness is all that woman has, and therefore nature under-

what despair is, or of the state's being one of despair. The despair
is mere passivity, a succumbing to external pressure; it comes
not at all from within as an action. It is due, if you will, to an
innocent misuse of language, a play on words, rather as when
children play at being soldiers, that words such as 'self' and
'despair' occur in the language of immediacy.

The *immediate* person (in so far as immediacy can occur
entirely without reflection) is specifiable only as soul, his self
and he himself a something included in the scope of the
temporal and the worldly, in immediate continuity with το
ἕτερον [*to heteron* – the Other], and it presents only an illusory
appearance of having something eternal in it. Thus the self co-
heres immediately with the Other – desiring, craving, enjoying,
etc., yet passively; even in its craving this self is in the dative

---

took to be her guardian. This is also the reason why femininity only comes
about in a transformation: it comes about when the infinite prudery transforms itself into feminine devotedness. But the fact that devotedness is
woman's nature, recurs in despair as the mode of the despair. In her
self-abandonment she has lost herself, and is only happy when having done
so, this being the only way she can be herself. A woman who is happy without
self-abandonment, that is, without giving of all her self, no matter what she
gives it to, is altogether unfeminine. A man also gives of himself, and it is a
poor kind of man that doesn't, but his self is not devotion (that being an
expression of the substantive self-abandonment of woman), nor does he
acquire his self through self-abandonment, as in another sense the woman
does; he possesses himself. He gives of himself but his self stays behind in the
form of a sober consciousness of self-abandonment, while the woman in
proper womanly fashion throws herself, throws her self, into whatever she
abandons herself to. If you take that away, then her self vanishes too, and her
despair is: not wanting to be herself. The man does not give of himself in this
way; but the second form of despair expresses also the masculine: wanting in
despair to be oneself.

So much for the relation between masculine and feminine despair. Still, it
must be remembered that we are not talking here of abandoning oneself to
God or the God-relationship, which we will deal with first when we come to
Part Two. In the relationship to God, where such a distinction between man
and woman vanishes, it is the case both for the man and for the woman that
self-abandonment is the self, and that the self is acquired through self-
abandonment. This applies to man and woman equally, even though no
doubt in fact the woman in most cases relates herself to God only through the
man.

case, as the child's 'me'. Its dialectic is: the pleasant and the unpleasant; its concepts: good fortune, misfortune, fate.

Now something *happens* to this immediate self; it *runs up against* something (or something runs up against it) which brings it to despair. Here it can happen in no other way, since the self is without any reflection. Whatever brings it to despair must come from outside, and the despair is mere passivity. That which for the immediate person is his whole life or, provided he has a modicum of reflection, that part of it to which he is peculiarly attached, is snatched away from him by 'a stroke of fate'. In short, he has, as he says, suffered a misfortune; his immediacy receives such a jolt that it is unable to reproduce itself: he despairs. Or, as one sees less often in real life but is dialectically quite acceptable, such despair on the part of immediacy arises through what the immediate person calls far too great a piece of *good* fortune. Immediacy is in this respect an extreme fragility, and every *quid nimis* [excess] that calls for reflection on its part brings it to despair.

So he despairs, that is to say, through a strange tergiversation and total mystification concerning himself, he calls it despair. But to despair is to lose the eternal – and of this loss he says nothing, he doesn't dream of it. To lose the earthly is not in itself to despair, and yet that is what he speaks of and he calls it despair. What he says is in a sense true, only not in the way he understands it. He is turned around and what he says must be understood backwards: he stands there pointing to something that is not despair, explaining that he is in despair, and yet, sure enough, the despair is going on behind him unawares. It is as though someone were standing with his back turned to the Town Hall and Court House, pointed straight ahead and said: 'There are the Town Hall and Court House.' The man is right, they are there – when he turns around. He isn't in despair, it isn't true, and yet in saying so he proves to be right. But he calls his state despair, he considers himself dead, a shadow of himself. None the less he is not dead; there is, if you will, still some life in the character. If everything suddenly changed, all the external circumstances, and his wish were fulfilled, then life would return to him, immediacy rise again to the surface, and he would begin life afresh. But this is the only way in which immediacy knows how to contest, all it knows: to despair and swoon – least of all does it know what despair is. It despairs and swoons and then lies quite still as though lifeless, a piece of artifice like 'playing dead'; immediacy is like certain lower animals whose only weapon or defence is to lie quite still and feign death.

However, time passes. If help comes from outside, life is restored to the despairer, he begins where he left off, he neither was nor became a self but now carries on living, merely in the category of the immediate. In actual life, if no help from outside is forthcoming, then what most frequently happens is something else. Although the character does in fact come to life, he says, 'I'll never be myself again.' He now acquires a modicum of understanding of life; he learns to imitate other people, how they conduct their lives, and proceeds to live as they do. In Christendom he is also a Christian, goes to church every Sunday, listens to and understands the priest, yes indeed, how they understand one another; he dies; for ten dollars the priest ushers him into eternity – but a self he neither was nor became.

This form of despair is: in despair not wanting to be oneself; or on an even lower level: not wanting in despair to be a self; or lowest of all: wanting in despair to be someone else, wanting a new self. Immediacy really has no self; it doesn't know itself and so cannot recognize itself either, and therefore usually it ends in fantasy. When immediacy despairs, it has not even enough self to wish or dream that it had become what it has not become. The immediate person helps himself in another way: he wishes he were someone else. One may readily convince oneself of this by observing immediate persons: in the moment of despair no wish comes more naturally to them than that they were or could become someone else. In any case, it is always difficult to refrain from smiling when one sees a despairer of this sort who, in human terms and despite his despair, is so very innocent. Such a despairer is in most cases infinitely comical. One imagines a self (and next to God there is nothing so eternal as a self), and then one imagines it occurring to a self whether it might not let itself be another – than itself. And yet a despairer of this kind, whose only wish is this craziest of all crazy transformations, is in love with the fancy that the change can be made as easily as one dons another coat. For the immediate person doesn't know himself; he quite literally only knows himself by his coat, he knows what it is to have a self – and here again we have the infinitely comical – only in externals. There could hardly be a more absurd confusion, for a self precisely differs infinitely from the external. When now, for the immediate person, all the external circumstances change and he despairs, then he goes one step further; he thinks like this, he wishes: 'What if I became someone else, got myself a new self?' Yes, what if he did become someone else – do you think he would recognize himself? There is the story of a peasant who had come barefoot to town and made so much money that he was able to buy himself a pair of stockings and shoes and still have enough left over to get himself drunk. On his way home in his drunken state he lay down in the middle of the lane and fell asleep. A carriage came along, and the coachman shouted to him to move aside or else he would drive over his legs. The drunk peasant woke up, looked down at his legs, and, not recognizing them because of the stockings and shoes, said: 'Go ahead, they aren't my legs.' So too when the immediate person despairs, it is impossible to draw a faithful picture of him which is not comic. Though I say it myself, even to speak in that debased language about a self and about despair is no mean artifice.

When immediacy is assumed to contain some reflection, the despair is somewhat modified. There is rather more consciousness of the self, and thereby also of what despair is and of one's state being one of despair. It means something for such a person to speak of being in despair. But the despair is essentially that of weakness, a passivity; its form is: in despair not wanting to be oneself.

The progress compared with pure immediacy becomes apparent immediately in the fact that the despair does not always come about through some jolt, through something happening, but can be brought on by the very reflection it contains in itself, so that, when it occurs, the despair is not mere passivity in the face of, and a succumbing to, the outside world, but is to some extent self-activity, an action. There being here some degree of reflection, there is also some degree of heed paid to one's self. With this certain degree of reflection begins that act of separation in which the self becomes aware of itself as essentially different from the environment and the external world and their effect upon it. But only to a certain degree. If the self which has some degree of reflection in itself now wants to take possession of the self, it may stumble upon one difficulty or another in the composition of the self, in the self's necessity.[40] For just as no human body is perfect, so neither is any self. Whatever this difficulty is, he recoils from it. Or something happens to him that infringes the immediacy in him more profoundly than in reflection. Or his imagination lights on some possibility which, if it came about, would then become that break with immediacy.

So he despairs. His despair is the despair of weakness, the self's passivity, in contrast to the despair of self-assertiveness. But with the help of the relative reflection he has in himself, and again distinguishing him from the purely immediate person, he makes an effort to protect his self. He understands that letting the self go is, after all, a conversion of property, so he will not be so apoplectically affected by the blow as the immediate person; he understands with the help of reflection that there is much that he can lose without losing the self; he makes concessions – he is capable of that – and why? Because to some extent he has separated his self from externalities, because he has a vague conception that there may even be something eternal in the self. But he struggles in vain. The difficulty he has stumbled on requires a complete break with immediacy, and he does not have the self-reflection or the ethical reflection for that. He has no consciousness of a self that is won by infinite abstraction from all externality. This self, naked and abstract, in contrast to the fully clothed self of immediacy, is the first form of the infinite self and the progressive impulse in the entire process through which a self infinitely takes possession of its actual self along with its difficulties and advantages.

So then he despairs, and his despair is: not wanting to be himself. On the other hand, the absurdity of wanting to be someone else certainly does not occur to him. He maintains the relationship to his self, reflection having attached him to his self to that extent. His relation to the self is like that of a man to his place of residence (the humour here is that the self does not stand to itself in a relation anything like as fortuitous as that of a man to where he lives), which may come to disgust him because of the smoke or whatever other reason. So he leaves it, but he does not move away, he does not establish a new residence, he continues to regard the old one as his address, he reckons the problem will pass. So too with the person in despair. As long as the difficulty remains, he dares not (as the saying so suggestively puts it) 'come to himself'; he does not want to be himself. But no doubt it will vanish, perhaps it will change, the sombre possibility will surely be forgotten. Until that time he comes only now and then, as though on a visit to himself, to find out whether the change has occurred. And as soon as it does he moves back in, 'is himself once more', as he puts it, though this simply means he begins where he left off; he was a self up to a point and went no further.

But if no change occurs, he helps himself in another way. He turns completely away from the inward direction, the path he should have followed in order truly to become a self. The whole question of the self in a deeper sense becomes a kind of false door in the background of his soul, with nothing behind it. He takes possession of what, in his language, he calls his self, that is to say, whatever aptitudes, talent, etc. he may have been given, all this he takes possession of but in the outward direction of what is called 'life', real life, active life. He deals very warily with the modicum of reflection he has in himself, lest this thing in the background comes up again. Then gradually he manages to forget it. In the course of the years he comes to think of it as well-nigh ridiculous, especially when in the congenial company of other capable and dynamic men with a sense and aptitude for real life. Charming! As it says in the novels, he has now been happily married for several years, a forceful and enterprising man, father, and citizen, even perhaps an important man. At home in his house his servants refer to him as 'himself'. In the city he is one of the worthies. In his conduct he is a respecter of persons, or of personal appearances, and he is to all appearances a person. In Christendom he is a Christian (in exactly the same sense that in paganism he would be a pagan and in Holland a Hollander), one of the cultured Christians. The question of immortality has frequently engaged him, and on more than one occasion he has asked the priest if there is such a thing, whether one would really recognize oneself again; which for him must be a particularly pressing matter seeing he has no self.

It is impossible to depict this kind of despair without a touch of satire. The humour of it is that he wants to talk of having been in despair; the awful thing is that the state he is in after having in his own mind conquered despair is precisely one of despair. It is infinitely comic that beneath all the practical wisdom that the world prizes so highly, beneath all that damnable profusion of good advice and wise sayings, of all that 'wait and see' and 'resign yourself to your fate' and 'leave it all behind', there is, ideally understood, total obtuseness about where the danger really lies, about what the danger really is. But this ethical obtuseness is, again, just what is so awful.

Despair over the earthly or over something earthly is the most common form of despair, and particularly in its second form as immediacy with a quantitative reflection in it. The more thoroughly reflected the despair, the more rarely it is seen, or

appears, in the world. But what this shows is that most people
have not yet gone particularly deep in their despair, not that
they are not in despair. There are very few people who live their
lives to any degree at all in the category of spirit. Yes, not even
many make so much as the attempt at that life, and of those who
do, most soon run away. They have not learned to fear, have not
learned what 'having to' means, regardless, infinitely regardless
of whatever may happen. Therefore they were unable to endure what already appeared to them to be a contradiction, but
which when reflected in the world around them appears far
more glaring – that to be concerned for one's own soul and to
want to be spirit looks from the world's point of view like a
waste of time, yes, an inexcusable waste of time which should
be punishable in civil law, in any case punished with contempt
and ridicule as a kind of treason against humanity, as a perverse
madness which manically fills out time with nothing. Then
there comes a moment in their lives – alas!, the best time of their
lives – when they begin to take the inward direction after all.
They come just about to the first difficulties, and then turn off. It
seems as though the road led to a dismal desert – *und rings umher
liegt schöne grüne Weide* [while all about lie pastures fresh and
green].[41] And so they try to get away, and soon they have
forgotten this – the best time of their lives – and, alas!, forgotten
it as if it were a piece of childishness. Also they are Christians –
reassured of their salvation by the clergy. This despair, as I have
said, is the most common; it is so common that this fact in itself
might explain the quite widespread everyday view that despair
pertains to one's youth, something which only occurs in
younger years but isn't found in the mature man who has
reached the age of discretion. This is desperately wrong, or
rather it is a desperate mistake which ignores the fact that most
people never really in all their lives manage to become more
than they were in childhood and youth: immediacy with a little
dash of reflection added. Yes, and even worse, it ignores the fact
that what it ignores is still just about the best one can say about
people, in view of the fact that what more often happens is far

worse. No, truly, despair is not something which only occurs in adolescents, something one grows out of with no further ado – 'as one outgrows illusion'. Though people don't do that either, even though they are foolish enough to think they do. On the contrary, one quite often comes upon men and women and elderly people who have illusions just as childish as those of any adolescent. But what is ignored is the fact that there are essentially two forms of illusion: that of hope and that of recollection. The adolescent's illusion is that of hope, that of the adult recollection. But precisely because the adult suffers from this illusion, his conception of illusion itself is also the quite one-sided one that the only illusion is the illusion of hope. And that is understandable. What afflicts the adult is not so much the illusion of hope as, no doubt among other things, the grotesque illusion of looking down from some supposedly higher vantage-point, free from illusion, upon the illusions of the young. The young person is illuded: he hopes for the extraordinary both from life and from himself. While as far as adult illusion is concerned, on the other hand, this is often found in the adult's recollection of youth. An older woman who has supposedly left all illusion behind is often found to be fantastically illuded, as much as any young girl, in her own recollections of herself as a young girl, of how happy she was then, how beautiful, etc. This *fuimus* [we have been],[42] which we so often hear from older people, is just as great an illusion as the younger person's illusions of the future; they lie or invent, both of them.

But desperate in quite another way is the mistake that despair belongs only to youth. In general, it is extremely foolish, and shows lack of insight into what spirit is – as well as failure to appreciate that man *is* spirit and not just an animal – to suppose it should really be such an easy affair with faith and wisdom that they just arrive over the years as a matter of course, like teeth, a beard and that sort of thing. No, whatever a human being comes to as a matter of course, and whatever things come to him as a matter of course, it is definitely not faith and wisdom. But the *will*

point is this, that in spiritual terms the human being does not arrive over the years and as a matter of course at anything. No idea could be more directly opposed to spirit. On the other hand it is very easy over the years and as a matter of course to leave something behind. And perhaps over the years one leaves behind that little bit of passion, feeling, fantasy, that little bit of inwardness one had, and comes as a matter of course (for such things come as a matter of course) to see life from the common-place point of view. This 'improved' condition, which has indeed come over the years, he now looks upon in despair as something good; he convinces himself easily (and in a certain satirical sense nothing can be more certain) that it could never now occur to him to despair – no, he has secured himself, he is in despair, spiritlessly in despair. Why do you suppose Socrates loved youth, if it was not because he knew man!

And if it should not so happen that over the years a person lapses into the most trivial kind of despair, it by no means follows that despair belongs only to youth. A person who really develops over the years, matures in essential consciousness of the self, may perhaps despair in a higher form. And if he does not develop essentially over the years, nor lapses entirely into triviality, that is, if in spite of being a grown man, a father, and grey-haired, he becomes what amounts to a young person, a youth, and thus retains some of the positive traits of the youth, then he will be liable also to despair, as the young person, over the earthly or over something earthly.

There may well be some difference between the despair of such an adult and a youth's despair, but if so it is not an essential, only a purely accidental, difference. The youth despairs over the future, as a *praesens in futuro* [present in the future]; there is something in the future he is not willing to take for his own, which means that he does not want to be himself. The adult despairs over the past as a *praesens in praeterito* [present in the past] which refuses to recede further into the past, for he is not so much in despair as to have succeeded in forgetting it completely. This past is perhaps even something which repentance should really have fastened on to. But for repentance to emerge, a person must first despair with a vengeance, despair to the full, so that the life of spirit can break through from the ground up. Despairing as he does, however, he dare not let it come to such a pass. So there he remains standing, time passes – but unless, in even greater despair, he manages to heal [hele] the past with the help of forgetfulness, instead of being a repentant he becomes the receiver [Hæler] of goods he has himself stolen. But essentially the despair of such a youth and of such an adult is the same; it never comes to any transformation in which consciousness of the eternal in the self breaks through, so that the struggle can begin which either intensifies despair to an even higher form or else leads to faith.

But then is there no essential difference between the two hitherto identically used expressions: to despair over the earthly (the totality) and to despair over something earthly (the particular)? Indeed there is. When with infinite passion the self despairs in imagination over something earthly, the infinite passion makes of this particular, this something, the earthly *in toto* [as a whole], that is to say, the totality concept is inherent in and belongs to the despairer. The earthly and temporal as such are precisely what flow out of each other into something, that is, into the particular. It is impossible actually to lose or be deprived of everything earthly, since the totality here is a category of thought. So the self first increases the actual loss infinitely, and then despairs over the earthly *in toto*. But once this distinction (between despairing over the earthly and despairing over something earthly) is to be applied essentially, an essential advance is also made in consciousness of the self. So this formula, to despair over the earthly, is a dialectical initial expression of the next form of despair.

(2) Despair of the eternal or over oneself

Despair over the earthly or over something earthly is really also despair of the eternal and over oneself, in so far as it is despair, for this is indeed the formula for all despair.* But the despairer depicted above was not aware of what, as it were, was going on behind him. He thinks he is in despair over something earthly, and talks constantly of what he despairs over, and yet his despair is of the eternal. For, after all, the fact that he ascribes such great value to the earthly, or even more, ascribes such great value to something earthly, or that he first of all makes of some earthly thing everything earthly and then ascribes such great value to the earthly, is precisely to despair of the eternal.

Now this despair is a significant step forward. If the former despair was despair in *weakness*, then this is: *despair over one's weakness*, while still remaining within the classification: despair as weakness, as distinct from β [p. 98] (defiance). So there is only a relative difference. This consists in the fact that the previous form has weakness's own consciousness as its final form of consciousness, whereas in this case consciousness does not stop there, but heightens itself into a new consciousness, namely consciousness *of* its weakness. The despairer himself understands that it is weakness to be so touchy about the earthly, that it is weakness to despair. But instead of now definitely turning away from despair in the direction of faith, humbling himself before God under his weakness, he engrosses

---

* And therefore it is linguistically correct to say: to despair *over* the earthly (the occasion), *of* the eternal, but, again: *over* oneself; for the latter is another expression for whatever occasions the despair, which according to the concept is always itself *of* the eternal, whereas what one despairs *over* can be so many different things. One despairs *over* whatever binds one in despair: over one's misfortune, over the earthly, over the loss of one's fortune, etc.; but *of* whatever, rightly understood, releases one from it: of the eternal, of one's salvation, of one's own strength, etc. In respect of the self, one says both to despair *over* and to despair *of* oneself, because the self is doubly dialectical. And this is the obscurity which, particularly in all lower forms of despair but also in almost anyone in despair, allows a person to see and know with such passionate clarity what he despairs *over*, while what his despair is *of* escapes him. The condition for his being healed is always this conversion to the *of* [*Omvendelse* – religious conversion, lit. about-turn, the 'about' here punned as 'of'. *Translator*]; and purely philosophically it could be a subtle question whether it is possible both to be in despair and to be quite clear about what one despairs *of*.

himself further in despair and despairs over his weakness. His whole point of view is thus turned around. He is now more clearly conscious of his despair, of the fact that he despairs of the eternal; he despairs over himself, that he could have been so weak as to attach such great significance to the earthly, and this now becomes his despairing expression for having lost the eternal and himself.

Here is the progression. First in the consciousness of the self, since it is impossible to despair of the eternal without having a conception of the self, of there being something eternal in it, or of there having been something eternal in it. And if one is to despair over oneself, one must also be conscious of having a self; and yet that is what one despairs over, not over the earthly or something earthly, but over oneself. Then, further, we have here a greater consciousness of what despair is, since despair is indeed loss of the eternal and of oneself. There is, of course, also more consciousness of one's state being one of despair. Then again, here the despair is not just a passivity, but an action. For when the earthly is taken away from the self and one despairs, it is as if the despair came from outside, even though it always comes from the self; but when the self despairs over this very despair, then this new despair comes from the self, indirectly-directly from the self, as a counter-pressure (reaction), thus differing from defiance which comes from the self directly. Finally, what we have here is, though in another sense, a further step forward. For just because it is more intense, this despair is in a certain sense closer to salvation. A despair of this kind is hard to forget – it goes too deep; but any moment the despair is held open, there is also a possibility of salvation.

None the less, this despair is still to be classified under the form: in despair not wanting to be oneself. As a father disinherits a son, the self will not acknowledge itself after it has been so weak. Despairingly it is unable to forget that weakness; somehow it hates itself, it will not humble itself in faith under its weakness in order to win itself back. No, in despair it will not, as it were, hear a word about itself, will have nothing to do with itself. But then neither can there be any question of being helped by forgetting, nor of slipping with the help of forgetfulness into the category of spiritlessness, so as to be a man and a Christian just like other men and Christians; no, the self is too much of a self for that. As doubtless often with the father who disinherited the son: the external fact only helped a little; it did not rid him of the son, least of all in his thoughts. As so often it helps little when the lover curses the despised (that is, loved) one, but almost intricates him the more, so it is for the despairing self with itself.

This despair is a level deeper in kind than that described earlier and is of a sort which appears in the world more rarely. That false door of which we spoke then, and which had nothing behind it, is now a real door though kept carefully closed, and behind it the self sits, as it were, keeping watch on itself, preoccupied or filling time with not wanting to be itself, yet still self enough to love itself. This is what is called being *reserved*.[43] And from now on we shall discuss this reserve, which is the direct opposite of immediacy and has great contempt for the latter.

But is no such self then part of actual life? Has he taken flight from reality into the wilderness, the monastery, the madhouse? Is he not a real person, fully dressed like others or going about as they in the usual kind of coat? Yes indeed! Why not? But this matter of the self he takes up with no one, not one soul; either he feels no urge to do so or he has learned to suppress it. Just listen to what he himself has to say on the subject: 'After all it's only purely immediate people – who spiritually speaking have come about as far as the child in its first stage of early childhood, where it lets everything out with such totally endearing unembarrassment – only purely immediate people can't keep anything back. This is the immediacy which often so pretentiously calls itself truth, honesty, being oneself, and has as much truth in it as a grown person giving way to a physical urge as soon as he feels it. Surely any self with even the slightest drop of reflection has some conception of what it is to restrain oneself!'

And our despairer then maintains sufficient reserve to keep every trespasser, that is, everyone, away from this matter of the self, while outwardly he is every bit 'a real person'. He has a university education, is a husband, father, even an exceptionally competent public servant, a parent to be respected, pleasant company, very gentle to his wife, solicitude itself towards his children. And Christian? Well, yes. He is that too. On the other hand, he prefers not to talk about it, though happy to note with a certain wistful pleasure that his wife occupies herself with religious observances for her own edification. Church he very rarely attends, because it strikes him that the majority of priests really don't know what they are talking about. He makes an exception in the case of just one particular priest, of whom he admits that he does know what he is talking about. But then there is another reason why he does not want to hear him – he is afraid it might lead him too far afield. On the other hand, he not infrequently feels the need of solitude; it is a necessity of life for him, sometimes like breathing, sometimes like sleep. Now the fact that it is more of a necessity for him than for others is also a sign that he has a deeper nature. In general, the urge for solitude is a sign that there is after all spirit in a person and the measure of what spirit there is. So little do chattering nonentities and socializers feel the need for solitude that, like love-birds, if left alone for an instant they promptly die. As the little child must be lulled to sleep, so these need the soothing hushaby of social life to be able to eat, drink, sleep, pray, fall in love, etc. It isn't only in the Middle Ages that people have been aware of this need for solitude, but also in antiquity there was respect for what it means; while in the never-ending sociality of our own day one shrinks from solitude to the point of not knowing to what use to put it except (oh! excellent epigram) the punishment of law-breakers. Yet it is true; in our own day it is indeed a crime to have spirit, so the fact that such people, the lovers of solitude, are put into the same category as criminals is just as it should be.

The reserved despairer lives on *horis successivis* [hour after hour], in hours which if not lived for eternity still have something to do with the eternal, occupied as he is with his self's relation to itself. But really he comes no further. When it is done, after the longing for solitude has been satisfied, it is then as though he goes outside – even when he goes into his wife and family or involves himself in their affairs. Aside from his good-nature and sense of duty, what makes him so gentle a husband, so solicitous a father, is the confession he has made to himself, in the inner recesses of his reserve, about his weakness.

If it were possible for someone to be privy to this reserve, and this person were to say to him, 'This is pride, really you are proud of your self,' the confession is hardly likely to be one he makes to another. When alone with himself he may well admit there was something to it, but the passion with which his self had grasped hold of this weakness will soon have him believe once more that it could not possibly be pride, since it is precisely his own weakness that he despairs over – as if it was not pride that put such immense emphasis on the weakness, as though it wasn't because he wanted to be proud of his own self that he found this consciousness of his own weakness unbearable. If one were to say to him, 'Here's a curious muddle, a curious sort of knot, for the whole sorry business is really due to how thought twists things; otherwise it is even quite normal. In fact this is just the path you should follow, you must go through with this despair of the self to get to the self. You are quite right about the weakness, but that is not what you are to despair over; the self must be broken down to become itself, just stop despairing over it' – if one were to talk to him in this way, he would understand it in a dispassionate moment, but the passion would soon distort his vision again, and so he turns once more in the wrong direction, into despair.

As was stated, despair of this kind is a rather rare occurrence. If it does not come to a halt at this point, merely marking time, and on the other hand the despairer undergoes no great upset which puts him on the right road leading to faith, then either such a despair will intensify itself to a higher form of despair and go on being reserve, or it will break through and destroy the outward disguise in which such a despairer has been living out his life incognito. In this latter case, a person despairing in this way will fling himself out into life, perhaps into the diversion of great enterprises; he will be a restless spirit whose life certainly leaves its mark, a restless spirit who wants to forget, and when the inner tumult is too much for him, strong remedies will be needed, though not of the kind Richard III uses to avoid having to listen to his mother's curses.[44] Or he will seek forgetfulness in sensuality, perhaps in dissolute indulgence; in his despair he wants to return to immediacy, but ever conscious of the self he does not want to be. In the former case, when the despair heightens, it becomes defiance; and now it becomes evident how much untruth there was in this business of weakness; it becomes evident how dialectically correct it is to say that the initial expression of defiance is precisely despair over one's weakness.

Nevertheless, let us in conclusion briefly look in once more on the reserved person who, pent-up in his reserve, marks time. If this reserve is maintained absolutely, *omnibus numeris absoluta* [perfectly in all respects], then suicide is the most likely danger. Of course, the common run of people have no idea what such a reserved person is capable of enduring and would be astonished if they knew. The danger facing the absolutely reserved person, then, is suicide. On the other hand, if he talks to someone, opens himself to even just one single person, in all probability he will feel himself so deflated, so let down, that the reserve will not result in suicide. A reserve of this kind, with an accessory, is a whole tone milder than the absolute case. So he will probably escape suicide. Nevertheless, it may be that just because he has opened himself to another, he despairs over that; it may strike him that it would have been infinitely preferable to have kept silent than to have someone privy to his despair. There are examples of reserve being brought to despair precisely through having acquired a confidant. Then it may still end in suicide. In fiction, the plot (assuming *poetice* [poetically] the hero to be, for example, some king or emperor) could turn on the confidant being put to death. Thus one might imagine a demonic tyrant who felt the need to confide in someone about his torment and to that end consumed a whole succession of people, since to be his confidant was certain death; as soon as the tyrant had unburdened himself to him he was put to death. It would be a writer's task to portray in a demonic character this way of resolving the agonizing self-contradiction of not being able to do without a confidant and not being able to have one.

β. The despair of wanting in despair to be oneself – defiance

Just as it was pointed out that the despair in α. [p. 80] might be called feminine despair, so this one might be called masculine. Compared with the preceding despair it is therefore also despair viewed from the point of view of spirit. But this means that masculinity also belongs essentially to the category of spirit, while femininity is a lower synthesis.

The despair described in α(2) [p. 91] was over one's weakness, the despairer does not want to be himself. But if, dialectically, just one single further step is taken, then the person who despairs in this way comes to the consciousness of why he does not want to be himself. Then the whole thing turns around, defiance is there, just because now he wants in despair to be himself.

First comes despair over the earthly or something earthly, then despair of the eternal over oneself. Then comes the defiance, which is really despair by means of the eternal, the despairing misuse of the eternal in the self to want in despair to be oneself. But just because it is despair by means of the eternal, it is in one sense very close to the truth. And just because it is very close to the truth, it is infinitely far away. The despair which is the corridor to faith is also due to the help of the eternal; through the eternal the self has the courage to lose itself in order to win itself. But here it will not begin by losing itself; it wants, on the contrary, to be itself.

In this form of despair we have now a raising of the level of consciousness of the self, that is increased consciousness of what despair is, and of one's state being one of despair. Here despair is conscious of itself as an activity; it comes not from the outside in the form of a passivity in the face of external pressure, but directly from the self. And that means that defiance, compared with despair over one's weakness, is indeed a new qualification.

In order to want in despair to be oneself, there must be consciousness of an infinite self. However, this infinite self is really only the most abstract form of the self, the most abstract possibility of the self. And it is this self the despairer wants to be, severing the self from any relation to the power which has established it, or severing it from the conception that there is such a power. By means of this infinite form, the self wants in despair to rule over himself, or create himself, make this self the self he wants to be, determine what he will have and what he will not have in his concrete self. His concrete self, or his concreteness, has indeed necessity and limits, is this quite definite thing, with these aptitudes, predispositions, etc., in this concrete set of circumstances, etc. But by means of the infinite form, the negative self, he wants first to undertake to refashion the whole thing in order to get out of it a self such as he wants, produced by means of the infinite form of the negative self – and it is in this way he wants to be himself. That is to say, he wants to begin a little earlier than other people, not at and with the beginning, but 'in the beginning';[45] he does not want to don his own self, does not want to see his task in his given self, he wants, by virtue of being the infinite form, to construct it himself.

If a common name were to be applied to this form of despair, one might call it Stoicism, though not just in the sense of the sect. And to throw further light on this kind of despair, it is best to distinguish between an active and a passive self, and to show how the self relates to itself when it is active, and how it relates to itself when it is passive and acted upon, so that the formula always is: wanting in despair to be oneself.

If the despairing self is *active*, then really it is constantly relating to itself only experimentally, no matter what it undertakes, however great, however amazing and with whatever perseverance. It recognizes no power over itself; therefore in the final instance it lacks seriousness and can only conjure forth an appearance of seriousness, even when it bestows upon its experiments its greatest possible attention. That is a specious seriousness. As with Prometheus' theft of fire from the gods, this is stealing from God the thought – which is seriousness – that God takes notice of one, in place of which the despairing self is content with taking notice of itself, which is meant to bestow infinite interest and significance on its enterprises, and which is exactly what makes them experiments. For even if this self does not go so far in its despair as to become an experimental god, no derived self, by taking notice of itself, can make itself more than it already is; it remains itself from first to last, in its self-duplication it still becomes neither more nor less than the self. In so far as the self, in the despairing endeavour of its wish to be itself, works its way into the exact opposite, it really becomes no self. In the whole dialectic in which it acts there is nothing firm; at no moment does what the self amounts to stand firm, that is eternally firm. The negative form of the self exerts the loosening as much as the binding power;[46] it can, at any moment, start quite arbitrarily all over again and, however far an idea is pursued in practice, the entire action is contained within a hypothesis. So, far from the self succeeding increasingly in being itself, it becomes increasingly obvious that it is a hypothetical self. The self is its own master, absolutely (as one says) its own master; and exactly this is the despair, but also what it regards as its pleasure and joy. But it is easy on closer examination to see that this absolute ruler is a king without a country, that really he rules over nothing; his position, his kingdom, his sovereignty, are subject to the dialectic that rebellion is legitimate at any moment. Ultimately it is arbitrarily based upon the self itself.

Consequently, the despairing self is forever building only

castles in the air, and is always only fencing with an imaginary opponent. All these experimental virtues look very splendid; they fascinate for a moment, like oriental poetry; such self-discipline, such imperturbability, such ataraxy, etc. border almost on the fabulous. Yes, that they do for sure, and beneath it all there is nothing. The self wants in its despair to savour to the full the satisfaction of making itself into itself, of developing itself, of being itself; it wants to take the credit for this fictional, masterly project, its own way of understanding itself. And yet what it understands itself to be is in the final instance a riddle; just when it seems on the point of having the building finished, at a whim it can dissolve the whole thing into nothing.

If the despairing self is *passive*, the despair is still: to want in despair to be oneself. Perhaps, while taking his bearings provisionally from the concrete self, an experimenting self of this kind, who wants in despair to be himself, stumbles upon some difficulty or another, something the Christian would call a cross, a basic fault, whatever that may be. The negative self, the infinite form of the self, may begin by altogether rejecting this, pretending that it is not there, having nothing to do with it. But it does not succeed, this far its experimental abilities do not reach, not even its ability to abstract; in a Promethean way,[47] the infinite, negative self feels itself nailed to this restriction in its powers to dispose over its own property.[48] Accordingly, it is a passive self. How, then, does the despair that is wanting in despair to be oneself come to light?

Well, earlier we presented the form of despair that despairs over the earthly or over something earthly, understood as being basically, and manifestly, despair of the eternal, that is, as an unwillingness to be comforted and healed by the eternal, as placing such a high value on the earthly that the eternal cannot be any comfort. But not being willing to have hope in the possibility of the removal of an earthly need, a temporal cross, is also a form of despair. That is what the despairer who wants in despair to be himself is not willing to do. If he is convinced (whether it is really the case or his suffering only makes it seem to be so) that this thorn in the flesh* gnaws too deeply for him to be able to abstract from it, then he wants, as it were, to take eternal possession of it. It offends him, or rather, he uses it as an excuse to take offence at all existence; he wants to be himself in spite of it, but not in spite of it in the sense of without it (for that, indeed, would be to abstract from it, which is something he cannot do, or it would be the movement towards resignation); no he wants to spite or defy all existence and be himself with it, take it along with him, almost flying in the face of his agony. Have hope in the possibility of help, especially on the strength of the absurd, that for God everything is possible? No, that he will not. And ask help of any other? No, that for all the world he will not do; if it came to that, he would rather be himself with all the torments of hell than ask for help.

And to tell the truth, it is by no means so true, as is said, that it is self-evident that a sufferer will ask for help as long as someone can help him. It is far from true, though the counter-examples are not always cases of a despair as great as this. The fact of the matter is this: someone suffering has usually one or more ways in which he could wish to be helped. If then someone helps him, well yes, he is glad to be helped. But as soon as the question of being helped begins, in a more profound sense, to be serious, especially when the help is to come from a superior, or the most exalted of all – then comes this humiliation of having to receive

* Just as a reminder, one can also see, from exactly this point of view, that much in the world that glories in the name of resignation is a kind of despair: the despair of wanting in despair to be one's abstract self, of wanting in despair to have in the eternal everything one needs, thus being able to defy or ignore suffering in the earthly and temporal. The dialectic of resignation is essentially this: to want in despair to be one's eternal self, and then with regard to something specific in which the self suffers, not to want to be oneself, consoling oneself with the fact that this thing may disappear in eternity and so feeling justified in not taking it on in time. Although the self suffers under it [whatever it is], the self does not want to admit that it belongs to the self, that is, will not in faith humble itself under it. Resignation, considered as despair, is thus essentially different from wanting in despair not to be oneself, for it wants in despair to be itself, though with the exception of one thing, in respect of which in despair it does not want to be itself.

unconditional help, in whatever form, of becoming like a nothing in the hands of the 'helper' for whom everything is possible, or even just of having to give in to some other person, to give up being oneself as long as one is asking for help. Ah! indeed, there is much, even prolonged and agonizing suffering in this way of which the self does not complain, and which it therefore fundamentally prefers so as to retain the right to be itself.[49]

But the more consciousness there is in such a sufferer who wants in despair to be himself, the more the despair intensifies and becomes the demonic.[50] It usually begins like this: A self which in despair wants to be himself, suffers some kind of pain which cannot be removed or separated from his concrete self. He then heaps upon this torment all his passion, which then becomes a demonic rage. If it should now happen that God in heaven and all the angels were to offer to help him to be rid of this torment – no, he does not want that, now it is too late. Once he would gladly have given everything to be rid of this agony, but he was kept waiting, and now all that's past; he prefers to rage against everything and be the one whom the whole world, all existence, has wronged, the one for whom it is especially important to ensure that he has his agony on hand, so that no one will take it from him – for then he would not be able to convince others and himself that he is right. This finally fixes itself so firmly in his head that he becomes frightened of eternity for a rather strange reason: he is afraid in case it should take away from him what, from a demonic viewpoint, gives him infinite superiority over other people, what, from the demonic viewpoint, is his right to be who he is. Himself is what he wants to be. He began with the infinite abstraction of the self, and has now finally become so concrete that it would be impossible to become eternal in that sense, and yet he wants in despair to be himself. Ah! demonic madness; he rages most of all at the thought that eternity could get it into its head to take his misery away from him.

This kind of despair is rarely seen in the world; such characters are really to be found in the poets, the real ones, who always lend their creations this 'demonic' ideality, to use the word in a purely Greek sense. However, such despair does also occur in real life. What then is the corresponding externality? Well, there is no 'corresponding' externality, since a corresponding externality which corresponds to reserve is a self-contradiction. If it corresponds then it discloses. But here the external is entirely inconsequential, here where reserve, or what could be called an inwardness whose door has jammed, is so supremely the object of attention. The lowest forms of despair, in which there is really no inwardness, and where in any case there is nothing to be said about it – the lowest forms of despair have to be presented by describing or saying something about the externals of such despair. But the more spiritual the despair becomes, and the more the inwardness becomes a separate world for itself in reserve, the less consequence attaches to the external form under which the despair hides. But precisely the more spiritual the despair becomes, the more it attends with demonic cleverness to keep the despair enclosed in its reserve, and the more it therefore attends to neutralizing the externalities, making them as insignificant and inconsequential as possible. With despair it is like the troll in the fairy-tale who disappears through a crevice that no one can see. Precisely the more spiritual despair is, the more pressure there is on it to take up its dwelling in some externality behind which no one would dream of looking for it. This very concealment is something spiritual and one of the safety-measures for ensuring that it has, as it were, a reservation,[51] a world of its own reserved unreservedly for itself, a world in which the despairing self is restlessly and tantalizingly employed about wanting to be itself.

We began α.(1) [p. 80] with the lowest form of despair, which in despair did not want to be itself. The demonic despair is the most heightened form of the despair which in despair wants to be itself. This latter despair does not even want to be itself in Stoic self-infatuation and self-exaltation, not even in that no doubt mendacious way, but one that in a certain sense conformed to its own ideal of perfection; no, it wants to be itself in hatred towards existence, to be itself according to its misery; it does not even want defiantly to be itself, but to be itself in sheer spite; it does not even want to sever itself defiantly from the power which established it; it wants in sheer spite to press itself on that power, importune it, hang on to it out of malice. And that is understandable – a malicious objection must, of all things, take care to hang on to that to which it is an objection. Rebelling against all existence, it thinks it has acquired evidence against existence, against its goodness. The despairer thinks that he himself is this evidence. And it is this that he wants to be; this is the reason he wants to be himself, to be himself in his agony, so as to protest with this agony against all existence. As the weak despairer will hear nothing about what comfort eternity has in store for him, so too with this despairer, but for a different reason: the comfort would be his undoing – as an objection to the whole of existence. It is, to describe it figuratively, as if a writer were to make a slip of the pen, and the error became conscious of itself as such – perhaps it wasn't a mistake but from a much higher point of view an essential ingredient in the whole presentation – and as if this error wanted now to rebel against the author, out of hatred for him forbid him to correct it, and in manic defiance say to him: 'No, I will not be erased, I will stand as a witness against you, a witness to the fact that you are a second-rate author.'

PART TWO

Despair is Sin

A. Despair is Sin

Sin is: *before God, or with the conception of God, in despair not wanting to be oneself, or wanting in despair to be oneself*. Thus sin is intensified weakness or intensified defiance: sin is the heightening of despair. The emphasis is on: *before God*, or on there being the conception of God. What makes sin, dialectically, ethically, religiously, what lawyers would call 'aggravated' despair, is the conception of God.

Although there will be neither space nor opportunity in Part Two, and least of all in the present section, A. for a psychological portrayal, we can cite here the most dialectical borderline case between despair and sin, namely what could be termed a poet-existence inclined towards the religious, an existence which has something in common with the despair of resignation except for the presence in it of the conception of God.[52] Such a poet-existence, as may be seen from the conjunction and position of the categories, will be the most eminent poet-existence. From the Christian viewpoint, every poet-existence (all aesthetics notwithstanding) is sin, the sin of writing instead of being, the sin of relating oneself in imagination to the good and true instead of being it, or rather, of striving existentially to be it. The poet-existence here referred to differs from despair in that it has the conception of God, or is before God. But it is immensely dialectical and an impenetrable dialectical tangle as far as the extent of its obscure consciousness of being sin is concerned. A poet like this can have a very profound religious need, and the conception of God is a component in his despair. He loves God above everything, God who is the only comfort in his secret torment, and yet he loves the torment, he will not let go of it. He would be only too happy to be himself before God, but not in respect of that fixed point at which the self suffers; that is a point at which, in his despair, he does not want to be himself. He hopes eternity will remove it; but here in time, however much he suffers from it, he cannot

109

resolve to make it part of himself, to humble himself under it in faith. And yet he continues to relate himself to God, and that is his only salvation; it would be for him the greatest of horrors to be without God, 'it would drive him to despair'; and yet in fact, perhaps unconsciously, he allows himself poetically to falsify God just a little, rather more in the guise of the fond father who all too indulgently humours the child's 'only' wish. As a person who becomes unhappy in love turns into a poet and then blissfully extols the joys of love, that is how he became the poet of religiousness. He has become unhappy in religiousness; he realizes vaguely that what is required of him is to let go of this torment, that is, to humble himself under it in faith and take it on him as part of the self – for he wants to hold it at arm's length, but that means precisely keeping hold of it – though indeed he thinks it means (which as with every word of the despairer's is correct in reverse and so has to be interpreted backwards) ridding himself of it as far as humanly possible. But to take it upon himself in faith, that he cannot do, that is to say, really it is something he is unwilling to do, or his self comes to an end in obscurity at this point. Yet as with that poet's portrayal of love, so has this poet's portrayal of the religious a fascination, a lyrical flight like no married man's or Reverend's. Nor is what he says untrue. Not at all; his presentation is simply his happier, his better 'I'. In relation to the religious he is an unhappy lover, that is, he is not in the strict sense a believer; he has only the first requirement of faith: despair; and in it an intense longing for the religious. His conflict is really this: Has he been called? Is the thorn in the flesh a sign that he is to be put to extraordinary use? Before God, is it entirely in order to be the extraordinary one he has become? Or is the thorn in the flesh what he must humble himself under in order to attain the universally human? But enough of this. I can say with emphatic truthfulness, 'Who is it I'm speaking to?' 'Who bothers with psychological inquiries like this in the nth degree?' It is easier to understand those Nürnberg pictures painted by the priest;[53] they bear a deceptive resemblance to everyone, to the general run of people, and, from a spiritual point of view, to nothing.

Chapter 1

The successive stages in the consciousness of the self (under the aspect: before God)

Part One pointed consistently to a rising scale in the consciousness of the self. First there was unconsciousness of having an eternal self (C *B* (a) [p. 73]), followed by knowledge of having a self in which, however, there was something eternal (C *B* (b) [p. 77]), and under this latter again (α.(1) [p. 80], α.(2) [p. 91] and β. [p. 98]) there proved to be successive stages. This whole line of thought must now be given a new dialectical twist. The point is this. The progression in consciousness we have been concerned with up to now occurs within the category of the human self, or of the self that has man as its standard of measurement. But this self takes on a new quality and specification in being the self that is directly before God. This self is no longer the merely human self but what, hoping not to be misinterpreted, I would call the theological self, the self directly before God. And what an infinite reality this self acquires by being conscious of being before God, by being a human self that has God as its standard! A herdsman who (if this is possible) is a self directly before cattle is a very low self; similarly a master who is a self directly before slaves, indeed really he is not a self – for in both cases there is no standard of measurement. The child, who up to then has had only its parents' standard, becomes a self through acquiring, as an adult, the State as its standard. But what an infinite accent is laid upon the self when it acquires God as its standard! The standard for the self is always: that directly in the face of which it is a self. But this in turn is the definition of 'standard'. Just as it is only possible to add together items of one kind, so everything is qualitatively whatever it is measured by; and what is qualitively its standard of measurement [*Maale-*

stok] is ethically its goal [*Maal*]. And the standard and the goal are qualitatively what anything is, except in the state of freedom where, on the contrary, in so far as he is not qualitatively that which is his goal and his standard, this disqualification is one that a person must have brought upon himself, so that the goal and the standard remain, judicially, the same, making evident what he is not, namely, that which is his goal and standard.

There was much truth in that idea to which an earlier dogmatic theology so often resorted, but which a later that failed to understand or have any feeling for it so often objected to – there was much truth in the idea, even though it has occasionally been misused, that what made sin so terrible was its being before God.[54] From this people proved the eternity of hell's punishment and then later became cleverer and said: 'Sin is sin; it is none the worse for being against or before God.' Strange! Even lawyers talk of aggravated crimes; even lawyers distinguish between crimes committed against public officials and private citizens, prescribe different punishments for parricide and ordinary murder.

No, in this the earlier dogmatics was right: that the fact that sin was before God infinitely heightened it. Their mistake was to regard God as something external, and in effect to assume that God was sinned against only occasionally. But God is not something external like a police constable. What one must look to is the fact that the self has the conception of God and nevertheless does not do what God wants, that the self is disobedient. Nor is it just now and then that God is sinned against, since every sin is before God; or rather, what really makes human guilt into sin is that the guilty person was conscious of being before God.

The despair is intensified in proportion to the consciousness of the self. But the self is intensified in proportion to the standard by which the self measures itself, and infinitely so when God is the standard. The more conception of God, the more self; the more self, the more conception of God. Only when a self, as this particular individual, is conscious of being before God, only then is it the infinite self; and that self then sins before God. Therefore the selfishness of paganism, whatever else may be said about it, is not nearly so aggravated as that of Christendom, in so far as selfishness is also to be found here. For the pagan did not have his self directly before God. The pagan and the natural man have the merely human self as their standard. From a higher point of view, one may well be justified in seeing paganism as resting in sin, but the sin of paganism was really the despairing ignorance of God, the despairing ignorance of being before God; it is to be 'without God in the world'.[55] From another viewpoint, then, it is true that the pagan did not sin in the strictest sense, since he did not sin before God; and all sin is before God. Moreover, it is also in a sense quite evident that the pagan has many a time been helped to slip through the world without reproach just because his superficial Pelagian conception saved him.[56] But then his sin is a different one; it is this superficial Pelagian understanding of his. On the other hand, it is also quite evident that a strict Christian upbringing has oftentimes, in a certain sense, plunged a person into sin because the whole Christian view was too serious for him, particularly in an early period in his life.[57] But then again, in another sense this more profound conception of what sin amounts to is something that helps him.

Sin is: before God in despair not to want to be oneself, or before God in despair to want to be oneself. But is this definition, even if otherwise admitted to have its merits (the most important among them being that it is the only Scriptural definition, since the Scripture always defines sin as disobedience), not too spiritual? To this one must reply, first of all that a definition of sin can never be too spiritual (unless it is so spiritual as to abolish sin), for sin is precisely a specification of spirit. And second: why should it be thought too spiritual? Is it because it doesn't mention murder, stealing, fornication and such? But then is it true that it doesn't speak of these things? Are these not also a wilfulness against God, a disobedience that defies his commandments? If, on the other hand, in respect of sin one mentions only sins like these, it is so easily forgotten that everything, speaking humanly, can be more or less as it should be in these respects, and yet the whole life be sin, that notorious kind of sin: the splendid vices, a wilfulness which, either spiritlessly or shamelessly, remains, or wants to be, in ignorance of in how infinitely far deeper a sense a human self is under an obligation to obey God – in its every secret desire and thought, in its readiness to grasp and willingness to follow every slightest hint from God as to what is his will with this self. Sins of the flesh are the wilfulness of the lower self; but how often is one devil not driven out with the devil's own help[58] and the final condition not worse than the first? For that is just how things happen in the world: first a person sins out of frailty and weakness; and then, yes, then it might be that he learns how to take refuge in God and be helped by faith, which saves from all sin; but that is not what we are talking about here. So he despairs over his weakness and either becomes a Pharisee who despairingly manages to convert it into a kind of legal self-righteousness, or in despair plunges into sin again.

So there is no doubt that the definition embraces all imaginable and actual forms of sin. But there is also no doubt that it correctly brings out the crux, that sin is despair (since sin is not the unruliness of flesh and blood in itself, but the spirit's consent to it), and that it is before God. As a definition it is algebraic: to begin in this little work to try to describe the individual sins would be both misplaced and in vain. The main point here is simply that the definition embraces all forms, like a net. And that it does, as can also be seen if one tests it against its opposite, the definition of faith, the sure sea-mark which I steer by to hold myself on course throughout this whole work. Faith is: that the self in being itself and in wanting to be itself is grounded transparently in God.

But often enough this fact, that the opposite of sin is by no means virtue, has been overlooked. The latter is partly a pagan view, which is content with a merely human standard, and which for that very reason does not know what sin is, that all sin is before God. No, *the opposite of sin is faith*, which is why in Romans 14.23 it says: 'whatsoever is not of faith, is sin'. And this is one of the most crucial definitions for the whole of Christianity: that the opposite of sin is not virtue but faith.

Addendum
That the definition of sin includes the possibility of offence: a general observation about offence

The sin/faith opposition is the Christian one which transforms all ethical concepts in a Christian way and distils one more decoction from them. At the root of the opposition lies the crucial Christian specification: before God; and that in turn has the crucial Christian characteristic: the absurd, the paradox,[59] the possibility of offence. And it is of the utmost importance that this is demonstrated in every specification of the Christian, since offence is the Christian protection against all speculative philosophy. In what, then, do we find the possibility of offence here? In the fact that a person should have the reality of his being, as a *particular* human being, directly before God, and accordingly, again, and by the same token, that man's sin should be of concern to God. This notion of the single human being before God never occurs to speculative thought; it only universalizes particular humans phantastically into the human race. It was exactly for this reason that a disbelieving Christianity came up with the idea that sin is sin, that it is neither here nor there whether it is before God. In other words, it wanted to get rid of the specification 'before God', and to that end invented a new wisdom, which nevertheless, curiously enough, was neither more nor less than what the higher wisdom generally is – the old paganism.

One hears so much nowadays about people being offended by Christianity because it is so dark and dismal, being offended by its severity, etc. The best-advised course would be simply to tell them that the real reason why people are offended by Christianity is that it is too elevated, that its standard of measurement is not the human standard, that it wants to make man into something so extraordinary that he cannot grasp the thought of it. A quite elementary psychological account of the nature of offence will make this clear, and also show how infinitely silly is the behaviour of those who have defended Christianity by removing the offence; how stupidly or shamelessly people have ignored Christ's own directions, which often and so anxiously warn us against offence, that is, which point out that its possibility is there and is meant to be there. For if it were not, then it would not be an eternally essential component in Christianity, which would mean it was human nonsense of Christ, instead of removing it, to go about anxiously warning us against it.

If I were to imagine a poor day-labourer and the mightiest emperor who ever lived, and this mightiest emperor took it into his head to send for the day-labourer – who never had dreamed, and 'neither had it entered into his heart',[60] that the emperor knew of his existence, and who would therefore count himself indescribably happy just to be allowed to see the emperor, something he could recount to his children and grandchildren as the most important event in his life – if the emperor were to send for him and tell him that he wanted to have him as his son-in-law, what then? Then, humanly, the day-labourer would be somewhat, or very much, at a loss, shame-faced and embarrassed; humanly it would strike him (and this is the human aspect) as something exceedingly odd, something insane about which he least of all would dare say anything to any other person, since in his own mind he himself was already inclined to the explanation that the emperor wanted to make a fool of him – something his neighbours near and far would very soon be much occupied with, so that the day-labourer would be a laughing-stock for the whole city, with his picture in the paper, the story of his betrothal to the emperor's daughter sold by the ballad-wives.[61] Yet, being the emperor's son-in-law, that could well soon be a public fact, so that the day-labourer would have the evidence of his own senses to confirm whether the emperor was serious or whether he wanted merely to make fun of the poor fellow, make him unhappy for the rest of his life, and help him on the way to a mad-house. For here we have the *quid nimis* [excess] which can so infinitely easily turn into its opposite. Just a small kindness; that would make sense to the day-labourer, that would be understood in the market-town[62] by its highly respected cultured public, by all the ballad-wives, in short by the five times one hundred thousand people who lived in that market-town, which in pure numbers, to be sure, was even a very large city, while in regard to its grasp of and feeling for the extraordinary was a very small market-town – but this, becoming a son-in-law, that was much too much. And suppose now that it was not a question of a public fact, but a private one, so that its facticity could not help the day-labourer to be sure, but faith was the only facticity, and everything therefore entrusted to faith; a question of whether he had humble courage enough to dare to believe it (for brazen courage cannot help one to *believe*). How many day-labourers do you think would then have the courage? But the person who lacked that courage would be offended; for him the extraordinary would sound almost as though it were a mockery of him. He might perhaps honestly and openly admit: 'This sort of thing is too exalted for me. I can't make sense of it; to put it bluntly, it strikes me as foolishness.'

And now Christianity! Christianity teaches that this single human being, and so every single human being, whether husband, wife, servant girl, cabinet minister, merchant, barber, student, etc., this single human being is *before God* – this single human being, who might be proud to have spoken once in his life with the king, this human being who hasn't the least illusion of being on an intimate footing with this or that person, this human being is before God, can talk with God any time he wants, certain of being heard; in short this human being has an invitation to live on the most intimate footing with God! Furthermore, for this person's sake, for the sake of this very person too, God comes to the world, lets himself be born, suffers, dies; and this suffering God, he well-nigh begs and implores this human being to accept the help offered to him! Truly, if there is anything one should lose one's mind over, this is it! Every person who does not have the humble courage to dare to believe it is offended. But why is he offended? Because it is too exalted for him, because he cannot make sense of it, because he cannot be open and frank in the face of it, and therefore must have it removed, made into nothing, into madness and nonsense, for it is as if it were about to choke him.

For what is offence? Offence is unhappy admiration. It is therefore related to envy, but is an envy turned towards oneself, in an even stricter sense worst when it is turned towards oneself. The natural man's narrow-mindedness cannot bring itself to accept the extraordinary that God has intended for him, and so the natural man is offended.

The degree of offence then depends on how much passion a person has in his admiration. More prosaic people who lack imagination and passion, who are thus not properly fitted to admire, they too are offended, but they confine themselves to saying: 'I can't make sense of such a thing; I leave it be.' These are the sceptics. But the more passion and imagination a person has, the nearer he is in a certain sense, that is to say in terms of possibility, to being able to be a believer, *nota bene*, to humbling himself in adoration under the extraordinary, and the more passionate the offence, which in the end can be satisfied with nothing less than getting this exterminated, annihilated, trampled in the dust.

If you want to learn to understand offence, then study human envy, a study which I offer as an extra course, and fancy myself to have studied thoroughly. Envy is concealed admiration. A man who admires something but feels he cannot be happy surrendering himself to it, that man chooses to be envious of what he admires. He then speaks another language. In this language of his the thing he admires is said to be nothing, something stupid and humiliating and peculiar and exaggerated. Admiration is happy self-surrender, envy is unhappy self-assertion.

So too with offence: that which in an interpersonal relationship is admiration / envy, in the relation between God and man is adoration / offence. The *summa summarum* [sum total] of all human wisdom is this 'golden',[63] or perhaps rather this plated, *ne quid nimis* [nothing to excess], too much or too little spoils everything. This is bandied about as wisdom, rewarded by admiration; its rate of exchange never fluctuates, the whole of mankind guarantees its worth. Then if once in a while there lives a genius who goes just a little beyond, he is declared insane, by the wise. But Christianity goes a huge gigantic stride beyond this *ne quid nimis*, into the absurd: that is where Christianity begins – and offence.

One can see now how extraordinarily (supposing any extraordinariness remains) – how extraordinarily stupid it is to defend Christianity, how little knowledge of humanity it betrays, how it connives if only unconsciously with offence by making Christianity out to be some miserable object that in the end must be rescued by a defence. It is therefore certain and true that the person who first thought of defending Christianity in Christendom is *de facto* a Judas No. 2; he too betrays with a kiss, except his treason is that of stupidity. To defend something is always to discredit it. Let a man have a warehouse full of gold, let him be willing to give away a ducat to every one of the poor – but let him also be stupid enough to begin this charitable undertaking of his with a defence in which he offers three good reasons in justification; and it will almost come to the point of people finding it doubtful whether indeed he is doing something good. But now for Christianity. Yes, the person who defends that has never believed in it. If he does believe, then the enthusiasm of faith is not a defence, no, it is the assault and the victory; a believer is a victor.

This is how it is with the Christian and offence. That its possibility is present in the Christian definition of sin is quite right. It is: before God. A pagan, natural man, is very willing to admit that there is sin, but this 'before God', which is really what makes it sin, that for him is much too much. It seems to him (though in another way than that shown here) to make much too much out of being a human being. Just a little less and he is willing to go along with it – but 'too much is too much'.

Chapter 2

The Socratic definition of sin

Sin is ignorance. That, as is well known, is the Socratic definition, which like everything Socratic is always entitled to respect. However, with this Socratic view it is the same as with so much else Socratic – people have learned to feel an urge to go further. What countless number have not felt the urge to go further than Socratic ignorance! Presumably because they felt it impossible to stop there; for indeed, how many are there in any generation who can stand the strain of expressing universal ignorance existentially for even just one month?

I shall therefore by no means dismiss the Socratic definition on the grounds that one cannot stop there. But, with Christianity *in mente* [in mind], I shall use it in order to bring Christianity into relief – just because the Socratic definition is so genuinely Greek, and revealed here, as with any other definition that is not in the strictest sense Christian, that is, every intermediate definition, in its emptiness.

Now the defect of the Socratic definition is that it leaves it unclear how ignorance is to be more precisely understood, its origin, etc. That is, even if sin is ignorance (or what Christianity would perhaps rather call stupidity), which is in a sense undeniable, are we to take it to be original ignorance? Is the state of ignorance then that of someone who has not known, and has hitherto been unable to know, anything about the truth? Or is it an acquired, a later ignorance? If the latter, then sin must really consist in something other than ignorance; it must consist in the activity whereby a person has worked at obscuring his knowledge. But even assuming this, the intractable and very tenacious defect returns, in that the question now becomes whether at the moment he began to obscure his knowledge the person is clearly conscious of doing so. If he is not clearly conscious of doing so, then the knowledge is already somewhat obscured, before he gets going; and then again the question simply returns once more. If it is assumed, on the other hand, that when he began to obscure the knowledge, he was clearly conscious of doing so, then the sin (even if it is ignorance, in so far as this is what results) is not in the knowledge but in the will, and the question that has to be raised is about the mutual relationship of knowledge and will. With all such matters (and one could go on raising these questions for many days) the Socratic definition is really not concerned. It is true that Socrates was an ethicist, the first (in fact antiquity established unreservedly his claim to be the founder of ethics), as he is and remains the first of his kind. But he begins with ignorance. Intellectually the direction he goes in is towards ignorance, towards knowing nothing. Ethically, however, he understands ignorance in a quite different way, and so begins with it. On the other hand, naturally enough Socrates is not really a religious ethicist, even less a dogmatic one, as is the Christian ethicist. Therefore he does not really enter into the whole inquiry with which Christianity begins, into the *prius* [preceding state] in which sin presupposes itself, and which is given its Christian explanation in the dogma of original sin, a dogma which this inquiry will only touch on.

Therefore Socrates does not really come to the category of sin, which is without a doubt a defect in a definition of sin. How so? Well, if sin is ignorance, then sin does not really exist, for sin is precisely consciousness; if sin is ignorance of what is right, and one then does what is wrong because one does not know what is right, no sin has occurred. If that is to be sin, then it is assumed, as Socrates also assumed, that there cannot be a case of someone's doing the wrong thing knowing what is the right thing, or doing the wrong thing knowing it to be wrong. Christianly this is just as it should be, in a deeper sense quite in order; in terms of Christian interests it is *quod erat demonstrandum* [that which was to be demonstrated]. The very concept in which Christianity differs most crucially in kind from paganism is: sin, the doctrine of sin. And so, quite consistently, Christianity also assumes that neither paganism nor the natural man know what sin is; yes, it assumes there must be a revelation from God to reveal what sin is. It is not the case, as superficial reflection supposes, that the doctrine of the atonement is what distinguishes paganism and Christianity qualitatively. No, the beginning has to be made far deeper, with sin, with the doctrine of sin, which is also what Christianity does. What a dangerous objection it would be against Christianity, therefore, if paganism had a definition of sin which Christianity had to acknowledge was correct.

What then is the missing component in Socrates's specification of sin? It is: the will, defiance. Greek intellectuality was too fortunate, too naïve, too aesthetic, too ironic, too – too sinful – to be able to get it into its head that someone would knowingly refrain from doing the good, or knowing what is right, knowingly do what is wrong. The Greek mind posits an intellectual categorical imperative.[64]

The truth in this certainly ought not to be disregarded, and needs to be brought home in times like these which have lost themselves in so much empty, pretentious and useless learning, so that just as in Socrates's time, though even more so, people need to be Socratically starved a little. It is enough to drive one to both laughter and tears, no less the virtuosity with which many people are able to present the highest *in abstracto*, and in one sense quite correctly, than these protestations about having understood and grasped it – it is enough to drive one to both laughter and tears to see how all this knowledge and understanding exercises no influence at all on people's lives, and bears not the remotest relation to what they have indeed understood, but rather the direct opposite. The spectacle of this no less pathetic than ridiculous disparity causes one involuntarily to exclaim, 'But how in the world *can* they have understood it? Can it really be true that they have?' To this the old ironist and ethicist replies: 'Don't ever believe it, dear friend; they have not understood it, for if truly they had, then they would express it in their lives too, they would have practised what they understood.'

To understand and to understand; are these then two different things? Certainly. And the person who understands that – though not, be it noted, in the former sense – is *eo ipso* [by virtue of that very fact] initiated into all the secrets of irony. This is the contradiction that irony is concerned with. It is a very low form of comedy, and beneath irony's dignity, to see something comical in the fact that a person doesn't know something. Nor is there really any deeper form of comedy to be found in the fact that there have been people who thought the earth stood still – seeing they knew no better. Our age may well be in a similar position to another that knows more of physical nature. Here the contradiction is between two ages and there is no deeper point of coincidence. Such a contradiction is not essential, and so not really comical either. No, but that a person stands there and says the right thing – and so has understood it – and then when he acts does the wrong thing – and so shows that he has not understood it; yes, that is infinitely comical. It is infinitely comical that a person, stirred so to tears that the sweat pours from him as well as the tears, can sit and read or hear a discourse on self-denial, on the nobility of sacrificing one's life for the truth – and then, in the next second, *ein, zwei, drei, vupti*, eyes scarcely dry, he is in full swing – in the sweat of his brow and as best he can – helping untruth to triumph. It is infinitely comical that a person, with truth in his voice and mien, deeply affected and deeply affecting, can grippingly portray the truth, grandly look all evil, all the powers of hell, in the eye, with a confidence in his bearing, with boldness in his glance, his paces admirably measured – it is infinitely comical that almost the same instant, practically still in 'full fig',[65] he can leap aside at the least inconvenience like a faint-hearted coward. It is infinitely comical that a person can understand the whole truth about how wretched and petty the world is, etc. – that he understands it and then cannot recognize what he has understood, for practi-

cally the same moment he is off joining in the same wretched-
ness and pettiness, is honoured for it and accepts the honour,
that is, recognizes it. Ah! when one sees someone protesting
complete understanding of how Christ went about in the form
of a lowly servant,[66] poor, despised, mocked, and as the Scripture says: 'spitted on'[67] – when I see that same person taking so
many pains to seek refuge in the place where in worldliness it is
good to be, setting himself up as securely as possible, when I see
him so anxiously avoiding – as if his life depended on it – every
unfavourable breath of wind from right or left, so blissful, so
utterly blissful, so jubilant, yes, to round it off, so jubilant that he
even emotionally thanks God for it – for being honoured and
respected by everyone,[68] everyone; then I have often said to
myself, 'Socrates, Socrates, Socrates, how could it be possible for
this person to have understood what he claims to have understood?' I have spoken in this way; I have also wished that
Socrates were right, for Christianity does strike me, after all, as
being too severe; and it accords ill with my experience to make
such a person out to be a hypocrite. No, Socrates, you I can
understand; you make him into a joker, a kind of merry fellow,
you make him an object of amusement; you have nothing
against – you even approve – my preparing and serving him up
as something comical – that is to say, if I do it well.

Socrates, Socrates, Socrates! Yes, one may well invoke your
name three times; it would not be too much to invoke it ten
times if that could be of any help. People think the world needs a
republic, and they think it needs a new social order, and a new
religion, but it never occurs to anyone that what the world
really needs, confused as it is by much learning, is a Socrates.
And yet, naturally, if anyone were to think of it, let alone if
many were to do so, there would be that much less need for
him. What a delusion needs most is always what it thinks of
least – naturally, since otherwise it would not be a delusion.

So an ethical-ironical correction like this could be what our
age sorely needs, and perhaps really the only thing it needs, for
it is obviously what it thinks of least. Instead of going further

than Socrates, our most urgent need has now become simply this Socratic, 'to understand and to understand are two different things' – not as an established formula that in the end helps people in their deepest misery, since that is exactly to abolish the distinction between understanding and understanding, but as the ethical grasp of the everydayness of life.

The Socratic definition covers itself as follows. When a person does not do the right thing, then neither has he understood it; his understanding is an illusion; his protestation of understanding is a misleading message, his repeated protestations that he'll be damned if he doesn't understand, a huge, huge distance away on the greatest possible detour. But then the definition is indeed correct. If a person does the right thing, then he surely doesn't sin; and if he doesn't do the right thing, then he hasn't understood it either. If he had truly understood it, that would soon have moved him to do it; it would soon have made him a sound-image of his understanding:[69] *ergo*, sin is ignorance.

But wherein lies the defect? It lies in the fact, which the Socratic principle is itself aware of and remedies, though only to a certain degree, that there is no dialectical specification appropriate to the transition from having understood something to doing it. It is in this transition that Christianity makes its start. By taking this path, it shows that sin lies in the will and arrives at the concept of defiance; and then to fasten the end very firmly, it adds the dogma of original sin – for, alas!, the secret of speculative understanding is precisely to sew without fastening the end and without knotting the thread, which is why it can wondrously keep on sewing and sewing, that is, pulling the thread through. Christianity, on the other hand, fastens the thread with the help of the paradox.

Purely ideally, where the actual individual person is not brought in, the transition occurs necessarily (indeed in the System everything comes about by necessity),[70] or, there is just no problem at all in connection with the transition from understanding to doing. This is the Greek mind (but not the Socratic, for Socrates is too much of an ethicist for that). And the very same thing is really the whole secret of modern philosophy. For what it says is this: *cogito ergo sum* [I think therefore I am],[71] to think is to be. (In Christian terms, on the other hand, it goes: 'As thou hast believed, so be it done unto thee', or 'As thou believest, so art thou';[72] to *believe* is to be.) From which one sees that modern philosophy is neither more nor less than paganism. But still, this is not the worst of it, for kinship with Socrates isn't exactly the meanest position to be in. What is altogether un-Socratic in modern philosophy is that it imagines, and would have us imagine, that it is Christianity.

In the actual world, on the other hand, where we do bring in the individual person, there is this tiny little transition from having understood something to doing it; it is not always *cito citissime* [very quick]; it is not (if for want of a philosophical term, I may say it in German) *geschwind wie der Wind* [with the speed of the wind]. On the contrary, a very lengthy story begins at this point.

In the life of spirit there is no standing still [*Stilstand*] (really there is no state of affairs [*Tilstand*] either, everything is actualization); if a person does not do what is right the very second he knows it is the right thing to do – then, for a start, the knowledge comes off the boil. Next comes the question of what the will thinks of the knowledge. The will is dialectical and has underneath it the whole of man's lower nature. If it doesn't like the knowledge, it doesn't immediately follow that the will goes and does the opposite of what was grasped in knowing – such strong contrasts are presumably rare; but then the will lets some time pass; there is an interim called 'We'll look into it tomorrow.' During all this the knowing becomes more and more obscured, and the lower nature more and more victorious. For, alas!, the good must be done immediately, directly it is known (and that is why in pure ideality the transition from thinking to being occurs so easily, for there everything happens immediately), but the lower nature has its strength in dragging things out. Gradually the will ceases to object to this happening; it practically winks at it. And then when the knowing has

126

become duly obscured, the will and the knowing can better understand one another. Eventually they are in entire agreement, since knowing has now deserted to the side of the will and allows it to be known that what the will wants is quite right. And this is perhaps how a large number of people live: they contrive gradually to obscure the ethical and ethico-religious knowledge which would lead them into decisions and consequences not endearing to their lower natures. On the other hand, they expand their aesthetic and metaphysical knowledge, which is ethically a distraction.

Yet, with all this, we have still come no further than the Socratic; for as Socrates would say, if this happens, all it shows is that the person has not understood what is right. Which means that the Greek mind did not have the courage to say that a person knowingly does wrong, that knowing the right thing to do he still does the wrong thing. So it covers itself by saying: 'When someone does the wrong thing, he has not understood the right thing.'

Quite correct. And no *human* being can come further than that. No human being is able to say, of his own and by himself, what sin is, for sin is the very thing he is in. All his talk about sin is at bottom a glossing over of sin, an excuse, a sinful extenuation. For this reason, Christianity begins in another way, by saying that for man to learn what sin is there must be a revelation from God, that sin does not consist in man's not having understood what is right, but in his not wanting to understand it, and in his unwillingness to do what is right.

In fact, even about the distinction between not being *able* to understand and being *unwilling* to understand, Socrates tells us nothing; while on the other hand, he is the grand master of all ironists on the distinction between understanding and understanding. Socrates declares that the person who does not do the right thing doesn't understand it either. But Christianity goes a little further back and says: 'It is because he won't understand it, and that in turn because he is unwilling to do what is right.' Then, next, it teaches that a person does what is wrong (genuine

127

defiance) regardless of the fact that he understands the right, or omits to do the right regardless of the fact that he understands it. In short: the Christian doctrine of sin is nothing but insolent disrespect of man, accusation upon accusation; it is the suit which the divine as prosecutor permits itself to prefer against man.

Can any human being comprehend this Christian teaching? By no means; this too is Christian, that is, an offence. It must be believed. Comprehension is man's circumference in relation to the human; but to believe is man's relation to the divine. How then does Christianity explain the incomprehensible? Quite consistently, just as incomprehensibly by its being revealed.

Thus, in Christian eyes, sin lies in the will, not in the knowing; and this corruption of the will affects the individual's consciousness. This is perfectly consistent of it, for otherwise the question of how sin began would have to arise with respect to each individual.

Here again is the mark of offence. The possibility of offence lies in there having to be a revelation from God for man to learn what sin is and how deep it goes. The natural man, the pagan, thinks like this: 'Never mind, I admit I haven't understood everything in heaven and on earth. If there is to be a revelation, let it teach us about heavenly things. But that there should be a revelation to explain what sin is, that's the most ridiculous thing I've heard. I don't pretend to be a perfect human being, far from it, but I know it, and I am willing to admit how far from perfect I am. You think I don't know what sin is?' But Christianity replies: 'No, that is what you know least of all, how far from perfect you are and what sin is.' Note that in this sense sin is indeed ignorance in Christian eyes; it is ignorance of what sin is.

The definition of sin given in the previous chapter still needs to be completed. Sin is: having been taught by a revelation from God what sin is, before God in despair not to want to be oneself, or in despair to want to be oneself.

Chapter 3

That sin is not negative but affirmative[73]

That this is the case is something that orthodox dogmatics, and orthodoxy in general, have always contended, rejecting as pantheistic any definition of sin that made it out to be something merely negative: weakness, sensuality, finitude, ignorance and so on. Orthodoxy has seen, very rightly, that it is here the battle has to be fought or, as above, where the end is to be fastened; this is where one must stand firm. Orthodoxy has rightly seen that to define sin negatively is to make the whole of Christianity ineffectual. Therefore orthodoxy insists that there must be a revelation from God in order to teach fallen man what sin is and, quite consistently, that this communication must be believed, because it is a dogma. And naturally, the paradox, faith, the dogma, these three specifications form an alliance and agreement that are the firmest support and bulwark against all pagan wisdom.

So orthodoxy would have it. Through a strange misunderstanding, a so-called speculative dogmatics,[74] which to be sure has some dubious dealings with philosophy, thought it could *comprehend* this specification of sin, that it is affirmative. But if that is true, then sin is a negation. The secret of all comprehension is this, that the act of comprehending is higher than anything affirmative that it posits. The concept posits something affirmative, but the very fact of comprehending it is to negate it. Though partly aware of this, speculative dogmatics has known no other recourse than to throw in a detachment of assurances at the point where the movement occurs – hardly becoming in a philosophic science.[75] It is protested, each time more solemnly, with ever more oaths and curses, that sin is affirmative, that to say that sin is just a negation is pantheism and rationalism and God knows what else, though all of it something that speculative dogmatics repudiates and abhors – and then they switch over to comprehending it, to comprehending that sin is affirmative. In other words, it is only affirmative up to a point, not more so than that one can after all comprehend it.

And this duplicity on the part of speculative dogmatics is evident at another, though related, point. The category of sin, or how sin is defined, is crucial for the definition of repentance. Seeing this business of negating the negation is so speculative, there is nothing for it but to make repentance a negation of the negation – and so sin becomes the negation. It would certainly be gratifying, by the way, if some sober thinker could tell us how far this purely logical matter, which reminds one of logic's first relation to grammar (two negatives make an affirmative) and of mathematics – how far this matter of logic applies in the actual world, in the qualitative world; whether the qualitative dialectic isn't something altogether different; whether the 'transition' doesn't have a different part to play here. Indeed intervals simply do not exist *sub specie aeterni, aeterno modo*[76] [from the point of view of eternity, in the eternal mode] etc.; therefore everything *is*, and there simply is no transition. To *posit* something in this abstract medium is therefore *eo ipso* the same as to *annul* it. But surely, to look at actual life in the same way borders on insanity. It is also possible to say quite *in abstracto* that the *perfectum* [perfect tense] follows the *imperfectum* [the imperfect tense]. But if in actual life someone were to conclude from this that it followed of itself and immediately that something he had still to complete would be completed, he must certainly be mad. But so also with sin's so-called affirmative status, when the medium in which it is posited is that of pure thought. That medium is far too fugitive for the positing to be taken seriously.

Yet none of this concerns me here. I simply keep constant hold of the Christian principle that sin is affirmative – not as something that can be comprehended, but as a paradox which has to be believed. This, to my mind, is the right thing. Once all the attempts at comprehension are shown to be self-contradictory, the matter will appear in its proper light; it will then be quite clear that whether one is willing to believe it or not must be left to faith. I can very well comprehend (and this isn't at all too divine to be comprehended) that a person who for the life of him has to comprehend and can only form opinions on what would have itself to be comprehensible, will find this very meagre. But if the whole of Christianity hangs on this, on its having to be believed, not comprehended, on its *either* having to be believed *or* one's having to be offended by it, is it then so commendable to want to comprehend? Is it commendable, or isn't it rather either impudence or thoughtlessness to want to grasp what doesn't want to be grasped? If a king gets it into his head to want to be totally incognito and be treated just like an ordinary man, is it then, just because it strikes people as being in general a mark of greater respect to pay him royal homage – is it then right to do so? Or when a person does what he himself wants instead of paying deference, is it not precisely to assert oneself and one's way of thinking in the face of the king's will? Do you think the king would be pleased the more ingenuity such a person displayed in showing him the respect of a subject, if the king does not want to be treated in this way, that is, the greater the ingenuity with which such a person opposed the king's will? So let others admire and praise the person who pretends to comprehend Christianity. I regard it as a plain ethical task – perhaps requiring not a little self-denial in these speculative times, when all 'the others' are busy with comprehending – to admit that one is neither able nor supposed to comprehend it. Just this is no doubt what our age, what Christendom, needs: a little Socratic ignorance with respect to Christianity – but take note, a little *Socratic* ignorance. Let us never forget – although how many ever actually really knew or thought it? – let us never forget that Socrates's ignorance was a kind of fear of God and a worship of the divine, that his ignorance was a Greek rendering of the Jewish: The fear of the Lord is the beginning of wisdom.[77] Let us never forget that it was precisely out of reverence for the deity that he was ignorant, that, as far as was possible for a pagan, he kept watch as a *judge* on the frontier between God – and man – taking care that the depth of the qualitative difference between them was maintained, between God and man, that God – and man – *philosophice, poetice* etc. [philosophically, poetically] did not merge into one. This, please note, is why Socrates was the one who knew nothing, and this is why the deity recognized in him the one who was wisest.[78] But Christianity teaches that everything Christian exists only for faith. Therefore it wants to be precisely a Socratic, God-fearing ignorance, protecting faith from speculation through ignorance, taking care that the depth of the qualitative difference between God – and man – is fastened, as it is, in the paradox and faith, and that God and man, more dreadfully even than ever in paganism, do not thus *philosophice, poetice* etc. merge into one – in the System.[79]

It is only from one side, then, that there can be any question of throwing light on the fact that sin is affirmative. The account of despair in Part One pointed continually to an escalation. The expression of this escalation was partly a heightening in consciousness of the self, partly an arousal from passivity to conscious action. Together both expressions form, in turn, the expression of the fact that the despair comes not from the outside but from the inside. And it also becomes proportionally more and more affirmative. But according to the proposed definition of sin, the self infinitely heightened by the conception of God belongs to sin, and so in turn does the greatest possible consciousness of sin as an act. That is what is meant by saying that sin is affirmative; what is affirmative is precisely the fact that it is *before God*.

Furthermore, specifying sin as affirmative involves the possibility of offence in a quite different sense, namely as the paradox. For the paradox results from the doctrine of the atonement. Christianity proceeds first to set up sin so firmly as an affirmative position that human understanding can never comprehend it; and then the same doctrine undertakes to remove this affirmative position in a way that human understanding can never comprehend. Speculative philosophy, which talks itself out of the paradoxes, lops a little from both

132

sides and has an easier time; it makes sin not quite so positive –
and yet cannot swallow the idea that sin should be entirely
forgotten. But here too Christianity, which is the first discoverer
of the paradoxes, is as paradoxical as possible; it is as though it
were working against its own ends by setting up sin so firmly as
an affirmative position that now it seems perfectly impossible to
remove it – and then this very Christianity wants with the
atonement to remove it so completely that it is as though
drowned in the ocean.

Appendix to A

But then in a certain sense does not sin become a great rarity?
(The moral)

In Part One it was pointed out that the more intense despair
becomes, the more rarely it occurs in the world. But if sin is once
again this qualitatively intensified despair, must it not be quite
rare? What a surprising difficulty! Christianity subjects everything to sin;[80] we have tried to represent Christianity as rigor-
ously as possible; and now we get this strange conclusion, this
strange conclusion that sin does not exist at all in paganism, but
only in Judaism and Christianity, and there again only very
rarely.

Nevertheless that is how it is, but only in a certain sense.
'Having been taught by a revelation from God what sin is, before
God in despair not to want to be oneself, or in despair to want to
be oneself' is to sin[81] – and certainly it is rare for a person to have
developed so far, to be so transparent to himself, that this can fit
his case. But what follows from this? Yes, that is something one
may well pay heed to, for here there is a special dialectical turn.
It was not a necessary consequence of a person's not being in
a more intensive state of despair – from this it did not follow –
that he was not in despair. On the contrary; it was shown
precisely that most people, far, far the majority, are in despair,
but in a less intense state of despair. Nor is there any merit in

being in a higher degree of despair. Aesthetically it is an advantage, for aesthetically there is concern only for vigour But ethically the more intense despair is further from salvation than the less intense.

Likewise with sin: the lives of most people, characterized by the dialectic of indifference, are so far from the good (faith) as almost to be too spiritless to be called sin, yes, even almost too spiritless to be called despair.

It is admittedly very far from meritorious to be a sinner in the strictest sense. On the other hand, where in all the world could one find a real sin-consciousness (and note, it is this that Christianity wants) in a life so immersed in triviality and chattering mimicry of 'the others' that it can hardly – is too spiritless to – be called sin, and merits only, as the Scripture says, to be 'spewed out'.[82]

But this does not dispose of the matter, for the dialectic of sin simply catches you in another way. How does it come about that a person's life becomes so spiritless that it seems impossible to bring Christianity to bear on it at all, just as a jack (and Christianity uplifts just like a jack) can't be used where there is no solid ground, only marsh and quagmire? Is it something that happens to a person? No, it is the person's own fault. No person is born spiritless; and however many take it with them to the grave, as all they have got out of life – that is not life's fault.

But it has to be said, and as bluntly as possible, that so-called Christendom (in which all, in their millions, are Christians as a matter of course, so that there are as many, yes, just as many Christians as there are people) is not only a miserable edition of Christianity, full of misprints that distort the meaning and of thoughtless omissions and emendations, but an abuse of it in having taken Christianity's name in vain. In a little country, scarcely three poets are born to each generation, but priests are plentiful, many more than get appointments. The poet is said to have a call; in the minds of most people (and that means Christians) to be a priest it is enough to have passed an examination. And yet, a true priest is an even greater rarity than a true poet, and the word 'call' has originally a religious sense. But Christendom still thinks it is something to be a poet, and that there is something in the idea of a call. To be a priest, on the other hand, is in the eyes of the majority (and that means in the eyes of Christians) a notion destitute of any uplifting connotation, without the slightest mystery, *in puris naturalibus* [to be blunt] a livelihood. By a 'call' one means an official appointment; a call is said to be something one gets – indeed one also talks of having a call to give away.

Alas! the fate of this word in Christendom is like an epigram on all that is Christian. The misfortune is not that no one speaks up for Christianity (nor, therefore, that there are not enough priests); but they speak up for it in such a way that the majority of people end up attaching absolutely no meaning to it (just as the majority think that being a priest differs not at all from the altogether everyday activities of a merchant, attorney, bookbinder, veterinarian etc.). Thus the highest and holiest leave no impression at all, but sound like something that has now somehow – God knows why – become a matter of form and habit, as so many other things. What wonder, then, that – instead of finding their own form and habits indefensible – they find it requisite to defend Christianity.

But a priest should surely be a believer. A believer, yes! A believer, after all, is someone in love; indeed, when it comes to ardour, the most infatuated of lovers is as a stripling compared with a believer. Just picture a lover. You agree, don't you, that he'd be capable of speaking of his beloved day in and day out, as long as the day lasted, and the night as well? But do you suppose it could occur to him, do you think it would be possible for him, don't you think he would find it disgusting to speak in such a way as to offer three reasons for concluding that there was after all something to being in love – more or less as when the pastor gives three reasons for concluding that it pays to pray, as though the price of prayer had fallen so low that three reasons were needed to help give it some crumb of esteem? Or, and this is the same only even more absurd, as when the priest gives three grounds for concluding that to pray is a blessing that surpasses all understanding. Ah, priceless bathos!, that something which surpasses all understanding should be demonstrated through three *reasons*, which whatever else they're good for, do not surpass all understanding and, quite the contrary, must make it quite evident to the understanding that this blessedness by no means surpasses all understanding, for 'reasons', after all, lie within the scope of understanding. No, for that which surpasses all understanding – and for the person who believes in it – three reasons mean no more than three bottles or three deer! And now, to continue, do you think it would occur to someone in love to conduct a defence of his infatuation, that is, to admit that it wasn't the absolute for him, unconditionally the absolute, but that he thought of it along with the arguments against it, and the defence is based on these; that is, do you think he either could or would admit that he was not in love, let it be known that he wasn't? And if someone were to suggest to the person in love that he speak in this way, don't you suppose he would think that person mad? And if, besides being in love, he was also a bit of an observer, don't you think he would have a suspicion that the person who made this suggestion had never known what love is, or would have him betray and renounce his love – by defending it? Is it not self-evident, though, that to the person really in love it can never occur to want to offer three reasons in proof, or to defend it. For he is something more than all reasons and any defence: he is in love. And the person who does do that is not in love; he only makes himself out to be, and unluckily – or luckily – is so stupid as simply to let it be known that he is not.

But this is just how Christianity is spoken of – by believing priests; Christianity is either 'defended' or translated into 'the reasons', if there isn't also some dabbling at 'comprehending' it speculatively. It is called preaching, and it is even taken in Christendom to be a great thing that there is such preaching and that someone listens to it. It is for this very reason (and here we have the proof) that far from Christendom being what it calls itself, the lives of most people are, from a Christian point of view, still too spiritless to be called sin in a strict Christian sense.

B. The Continuation of Sin

Being in a state of sin is always new sin; or as it may be, and in the following will be, more precisely expressed: being in a state of sin is the new sin, it is the sin. The sinner may think this exaggerated: at most he acknowledges that every actual new sin is a new sin. But eternity, which keeps his account, must enter the state of sin as a new sin. There are only two columns and 'whatsoever is not of faith, is sin'.[83] Every unrepented sin is a new sin; and every moment it is unrepented is new sin. But how rare is the person who has continuity with respect to his consciousness of himself! As a rule, people are only occasionally conscious, conscious of the major decisions, and the everyday is not registered at all. They are spirit after a fashion once a week for an hour – which is of course a rather brutish way of being spirit. Yet eternity is the essential continuity, and demands this continuity of man, that he be conscious of himself as spirit and have faith. The sinner, on the other hand, is so much in the grip of sin that he has no conception of its totality and has strayed on to the road to destruction.[84] He registers only every particular new sin, which gives him as it were some extra momentum along that road to destruction, just as though he had not been proceeding in that direction the moment before and with all the momentum of his previous sins. So natural has sin become for him, or so much his second nature, that he finds the everyday quite in order and is given pause only for a moment, each time a new sin as it were adds to his momentum. In his destruction he is blind to the fact that instead of his life having the essential continuity of the eternal, by being before God in faith, it has the continuity of sin.

But 'continuity' of sin; is sin not precisely non-continuity? Here we have it again, this idea of sin's being something negative to which one can never gain entitlement, just as one cannot acquire a title to stolen goods, sin as a negation, or a vain attempt at self-constitution which, under all the agony of its powerless defiance in despair, proves beyond its powers. Yes, that is how speculation would have it, but in Christian terms sin is (and this has to be believed since it is the paradox which no man can comprehend) a reality which develops by itself an increasingly affirmative continuity.

Also the law for the growth of this continuity differs from that of a debt or a negation. A debt does not grow by not being paid back, it grows every time it is increased. But sin grows every moment one fails to get out of it. Far from being correct in thinking that only every new sin increases the sin, it is his being in a state of sin that, in Christian terms, puts the sinner in the greater sin, it *is* the new sin. We even have a proverb which says that to err is human while to remain in error is of the devil. But the Christian understanding of this proverb is surely rather different. Only to take sporadic note of the new sin and skip what lies in between, between the particular sinnings, is as superficial a way of looking at it as to suppose a railway train only moved each time the locomotive puffed. No, this puff, and the propulsion that follows, is not what one should really be looking at, but rather the constant speed at which the locomotive runs and from which the puffing proceeds. Likewise with sin. In the deepest sense, the being in a state of sin is the sin, the particular sins are not the continuation of sin, they are expressions of its continuation. In the particular new sins the speed of sin merely becomes more apparent to the eye.

The being in sin is a worse sin than the particular sins; it is the sin. And in this sense it is true that the state of sin is the continuation of sin, is a new sin. This is generally understood in another way, as one sin's giving birth to a new one. But that the being in sin is a new sin is something which goes much deeper than that. It is a psychological master-stroke that Shakespeare has Macbeth say (Act III, Scene 2): 'Things bad begun make strong themselves by ill.'[85] In other words, sin has an inner consistency and in this consistency of evil it also has a certain strength. But one will never come to see it in this way if one only looks at the particular sins.

Most people, to be sure, live in all too little consciousness of themselves to have any conception of consistency; that is, they do not exist *qua* spirit. Their lives, whether with a certain childlike and endearing naïvety, or with empty-mindedness, are made up from a bit of action here, a bit of incident there, this and that. One moment they are doing something good, the next something wrong again and so on all over again. They can be in despair for an afternoon, maybe three weeks, but then they are in good cheer once more, and after that in despair again for a whole day. They so to speak join in life's game but never have the experience of putting everything together, never come to a conception of an infinite consistency in themselves. Therefore they talk to one another only of what is particular: particular good deeds, particular sins.

Every existence which is in the category of spirit, even if only on its own account, has an internal consistency and a consistency of something higher, at least an idea. But then, a person of this kind infinitely fears any inconsistency, for he has an infinite conception of what the consequence can be: that he can be torn out of the totality in which he has his life. The slightest inconsistency is an enormous loss, for it means that he loses that consistency. At that very moment perhaps the spell is broken, the mysterious power which bound all his powers in harmony is exhausted, the spring loses its tension, perhaps the whole becomes a chaos in which, to its distress, the powers of the self rebel against each other, a chaos in which no internal agreement, no momentum, no impetus is to be found. The enormous machine whose consistency made its iron strength so compliant, which made it so supple in all its power, is in a state of disorder; and the better, the more imposing the machine, the more fearful the mess. The believer who, as such, rests in and has his life in the consistency of the good, is infinitely fearful of even the slightest sin; for he has infinitely much to lose. Immediate persons, people who are childlike or childish, have nothing total to lose; they always lose and win things in detail, something in particular.

THE SICKNESS UNTO DEATH

But, as with the believer, so also with his counterpart, the demonic, with respect to the internal consistency of sin. As a drunkard keeps himself continually intoxicated from day to day, for fear of stopping and the mental distress that would follow and the possible consequences if he should one day become quite sober, so too with the demonic. Indeed, also the good man who, if approached enticingly with a seductive portrayal of sin, would beg, 'Tempt me not!', provides exact parallels to a demonic person. Face to face with someone stronger in the good, who represents the good to him in its blessed sublimity, the demonic person can beg for mercy, tearfully beg the other not to speak to him, not, as he would put it, to make him weak. Precisely because he has an internal consistency and a consistency of evil, the demonic person, too, has a totality to lose. One single moment outside his consistency, one single dietetic imprudence, one single sideways glance, seeing and understanding the whole thing or even just part of it differently, just for a second, and perhaps he would never be himself again, so he says. That is, he has given up the good in despair; it couldn't help him in any way. But it can still disturb him, make it impossible for him ever to acquire the full momentum of consistency, weaken him. Only in the continuation of sin does he remain himself; it is only in this that he lives, has the impression of himself. But what does this mean? It means that in the depths to which he has sunk it is his state of sin which holds him together, wickedly strengthening him with its consistency; it is not the particular new sin which – yes, how dreadfully crazy! – 'helps' him; the particular new sin is simply the expression of the state of sin, which is really the sin.

Thus by 'the continuation of sin', now to be discussed, we are thinking not so much of the particular new sins, as of the state of sin which in turn becomes the internal intensification of sin, a remaining in the state of sin in the consciousness thereof. So, here as elsewhere, the law of movement for the intensification is: inwards, at an ever higher level of consciousness.

A

The sin of despairing over one's sin

Sin is despair; the intensification is the new sin of despairing over one's sin. It is easy to see that it is indeed a matter of intensification. It isn't a new sin, as when the person who once stole a hundred dollars another time steals a thousand. No, we are not talking here of particular sins; the state of sin is the sin and this is intensified in a new consciousness.

To despair over one's own sin is the expression of sin's having become or being about to become internally consistent. It wants nothing to do with the good, won't be so weak as even to listen to other talk just once in a while. No, it wants to listen only to itself, to have to do only with itself, be shut in with itself, yes, place itself inside one enclosure more and by despairing over sin protect itself against every assault or aspiration of the good. It is conscious of having hacked down the bridge behind it and of thus being as inaccessible to the good as the good is to it; so that even if in a weak moment it wanted the good, that would still not be possible. Sin is itself separation from the good, but despair over sin is separation a second time. Naturally, this extorts from sin the utmost powers of the demonic, gives it the ungodly hardiness or obduracy to look upon all that goes by the name of repentance, and all that goes by the name of grace, not merely as empty and meaningless, but as its enemy, as what more than anything must be guarded against, exactly as the good guards itself against temptation. Understood in this way, Mephistopheles says (in *Faust*)[86] quite correctly that there is nothing more pitiful than a devil in despair. For here despair has to be understood as a willingness to weaken oneself so far as to hearken to anything at all concerning repentance and grace. To characterize the heightening that occurs between sin and despair over sin, one could say that the former breaks with the good and the latter with repentance.

Despair over sin is an attempt to keep going by sinking even deeper. As the balloonist climbs by casting off weights, the despairer sinks by more and more determinedly casting off all good (for the weight of the good is uplifting); he sinks though in the belief, to be sure, that he is rising – and indeed he does become lighter. Sin itself is the struggle of despair, but when energy is exhausted there has to be a new intensification, a new demonic withdrawal into oneself, and that is despair over sin. It is a step forward, a heightening of the demonic, and of course a deeper absorption in sin. It is an attempt to give to sin some backbone and engagement as a power by its being now for ever decided to hear nothing of repentance, nothing of grace. And yet despair over sin is conscious precisely of its own emptiness, of its having nothing whatever to live on, not even a self-image. The line Shakespeare gives to Macbeth (Act II, Scene 1) is a master-stroke of psychology: 'For from this instant [having murdered the king – and now despairing over his sin] there's nothing serious in mortality: All is but toys: renown and grace is dead.'[87] What is masterly is the double stroke in the final words (renown and grace). Through the sin, in other words, through despairing over the sin, he has lost all relation to grace – and also to himself. His selfish self culminates in ambition. For now he has become king and yet, in despairing over his sin and of the reality of repentance and of grace, he has at the same time lost himself; he cannot keep it up, even for himself, and he is no closer to enjoying his own self in his ambition than he is to grasping grace.

In life (inasmuch as despair over sin crops up in life, but at any rate one runs across something people refer to in this way) people usually mistake this despair over sin, presumably because generally the world is preoccupied only with frivolity, mindlessness and prattle, and therefore as a rule becomes quite solemn and deferentially doffs its hat at the mention of anything deeper. Whether in confused unclarity about itself and its significance, or with a streak of hypocrisy, or through the cunning and sophistry present in all despair, despair over sin is not averse to giving itself out to be something good. Thus it is supposed to be the sign of a deep nature which therefore takes its sin so much to heart. Here is an illustration. When a person who has been addicted to some sin or other but over a considerable period has now successfully resisted the temptation – when this person has a relapse and succumbs again to the temptation, then the depression that ensues is by no means always sorrow over the sin. It can be something quite different; it might also, for that matter, be resentment of divine governance,[88] as if it were the latter that had let him fall into temptation and should not have been so hard on him, seeing that until now he had for so long successfully resisted the temptation. But in any case it is altogether womanish to regard this sorrowfulness as something straightforwardly good, without noticing anything of the duplicity present in all passionateness, which in turn presages the passionate person's understanding too late, sometimes almost to distraction, that he has said the very opposite of what he meant to say. Such a person protests, perhaps in ever stronger terms, how this relapse tortures and torments him, how it brings him to despair; he says, 'I will never forgive myself.' And all this is supposed to be the expression of how much good there is to be found in him, of how deep a nature he has. This is mystification. I deliberately introduced a cue: 'I will never forgive myself', an expression commonly used in just such a situation. And with this phrase one can straightaway orient oneself dialectically. He never forgives himself – but suppose now God would forgive him; then he might well have the goodness to forgive himself. No, this despair over sin, and especially the more it rages in the passionate expression that (as he least suspects) betrays him in saying never will he 'forgive' himself for having thus sinned (for this way of talking is close to being the opposite of a contrite heart that prays to God for forgiveness) – this, his despair over sin, very far from being a specification of the good, is a heightened specification of sin, the intensity of which is a deeper absorption in sin. The point is that, in the period of successfully resisting temptation, he became better in his own eyes than he is, he became proud of himself. It is now to this pride's advantage that the past be left entirely behind. But in the relapse the past suddenly becomes present. This reminder is something his pride cannot bear, and hence his profound distress, etc. But evidently the direction of the distress is away from God, a hidden self-love and pride, instead of beginning humbly by humbly thanking God that he helped him to resist the temptation for so long, acknowledging before God and himself that this is already far more than he deserved, and thus humbling himself under the memory of how he has been.

Here, as everywhere, we have what the old devotional books make so profoundly, so knowledgeably, so instructively clear. They teach that God sometimes lets the believer stumble and fall into some or other temptation – precisely to humble him and thereby confirm him the more in the good. The contrast between the relapse and what may be the significant step forward in the good is so humbling, the identification with himself so painful. The better a person is, the more profoundly painful the particular sin naturally is, and the more dangerous the least bit of impatience if he does not make the right turn. He may, perhaps out of sorrow, sink into the darkest melancholy – and an idiot of a minister be on the brink of admiring his deep soul and the power of good in him – as though this were the good. And his wife, yes, she feels deeply humble in comparison with such a serious and saintly husband who is able to grieve thus over sin. He may be still more deceptive in his talk; perhaps he does not say, 'I can never forgive myself' (as though he had perhaps previously forgiven himself for his sins – a blasphemy); no, he says that God can never forgive him his sin. And, alas!, this is only mystification. His sorrow, his concern, his despair are selfish (just as the dread of sin can sometimes in effect drive a person into sin through dread, because this dread is a self-love that wants to be proud of itself for being without sin) – and comfort is the last thing he needs, which is also why the vast number of grounds for comfort prescribed by the ministers merely make the sickness worse.

B

The sin of despairing of * *the forgiveness of sins (offence)*

Here the heightened consciousness of the self is knowledge of Christ, a self directly before Christ. First there came (in Part One) ignorance of having an eternal self; next knowledge of having a self in which, however, there is something eternal. Then (in the transition to Part Two) this distinction proved to be included under the self which has a human conception of itself, or which has man as its standard of measurement. The opposite of this was a self directly before God, and this formed the basis for the definition of sin.

Now comes a self directly before Christ — a self which nevertheless in despair does not want to be itself or in despair wants to be itself. For despair of the forgiveness of sins has to be referred to one or the other formula for despair: that of weakness or that of defiance; that of weakness which, being offended, does not dare to believe, and that of defiance which, being offended, will not believe. Except that here weakness and defiance (seeing that it is not just a question of being oneself, but of being oneself in the category of sinner, thus oneself in the category of one's imperfection) are the converse of what they normally are. Normally weakness is: in despair not wanting to be oneself. Here that is defiance; for here it is defiance not to want to be oneself, what one is, a sinner, and because of that to want to dispense with the forgiveness of sins. Normally defiance is: wanting in despair to be oneself. Here that is weakness, wanting in despair to be oneself, a sinner, in a way in which there is no forgiveness.

A self directly before Christ is a self intensified through the

---

* Note the distinction between despairing *over* one's sin and despairing *of* the forgiveness of sins.

stupendous concession God made, intensified by the stupendous accent that falls on this self because, also for its sake, God let himself be born, became man, suffered and died. As it was stated above, the more conception of God, the more self, so here it is: the more conception of Christ, the more self. Qualitatively, a self is what it has as its standard of measurement. That Christ is the standard, is the expression, attested by God, of what stupendous reality a self has. For only in Christ is it true that God is man's goal and standard, or standard and goal. But the more self, the more intense the sin.

The intensification of sin can also be shown from another side. Sin was despair; the intensification was despair over sin. But now God offers reconciliation in the forgiveness of sins. Yet the sinner despairs and the sin acquires an even deeper expression; it is now related in a way to God, and yet for the very reason that it is even further away it is even more intensely absorbed in sin. When the sinner despairs of the forgiveness of sins, it is almost as though he were directly putting pressure on God. There is something almost of the dialogue in this, 'No, there's no forgiveness of sins, it's an impossibility.' It has the appearance of a brawl. But the person must distance himself qualitatively further from God to be able to say this, and for it to be heard, and in order to fight *cominus* [at close quarters] he must be *eminus* [at a distance]. Such are the strange acoustics of the life of spirit, such its strange spatial arrangement. A person must be as far as possible from God for this No to be heard, even though the idea behind it is in a way to worst him. The most direct effrontery to God is from the greatest distance; to be barefaced to God one has to put oneself at a distance; one cannot be forward by going nearer, and being forward means *eo ipso* being far away.[89] Ah, how powerless is the human directly before God! When you cheek a man of high station you may be cast far away from him as punishment; but with God you have to go far away just to be able to cheek him.

In life, people mistake this sin (despairing of the forgiveness of sins) more often than not, especially since the ethical has been abolished and one rarely if ever hears a properly ethical word. Aesthetico-metaphysically, despairing of the forgiveness of sins is revered as a sign of a deep nature, more or less as though naughtiness were to be considered a sign of a deep nature in the child. Altogether, it is unbelievable what confusion has entered the religious sphere since the 'Thou shalt' was abolished as the only rule of conduct in man's relation to God. This 'Thou shalt' should be included in any specification of the religious; in its place the God-idea or the concept of God has been romantically exploited as an ingredient in human importance, so as oneself to become important directly before God. Just as one acquires importance in politics by belonging to the opposition, and eventually gives a government support just to have something to oppose, so finally one is loath to abolish God – just to become even more important by being the opposition. And all this, which was regarded in the old days with horror as the mark of wicked insubordination, has now become discernment, a sign of a deep nature. 'Thou shalt *believe*' is how it sounded in the old days, short and sweet, and as sober as can be – now it is a sign of genius and a deep nature not to be able to. 'Thou shalt believe in the forgiveness of sins' is how it went, and the only commentary on that went, 'It will go ill with you if you cannot do so; for what one shall do, one can do'[90] – it is now a sign of genius and a deep nature not to be able to believe in it. To what a splendid pass Christendom has brought it! If not a word were heard about Christianity, men would not be so conceited – something paganism, for that matter, has never been either; but because of their being un-Christianly in the air, these Christian concepts are put to the most aggravatedly impertinent use, if not also misused in some other but equally shameless way. For is it not indeed epigrammatic that though in paganism it was bad manners to swear, here at home in Christendom, on the contrary, it is quite proper; that while paganism mentioned God's name with some awe, with a healthy respect for the mysterious, and most often with great solemnity, in Christendom God's name is the word that occurs most often in everyday speech, and incontestably the word to which least meaning is attached and that is used with least care, because this pitiable revealed God (who was so incautious and imprudent as to make himself visible instead of staying in hiding, as those in superior circles mostly always do) has become all too well known a personage to the population at large, who now do him an incalculably great service by going once in a while to church, where they are also commended by the priest who thanks them on God's behalf for the honour of the visit, and confers on them the title of piety, while making a few gibes at the expense of those who never do God the honour of going to church.

The sin of despairing of the forgiveness of sins is *offence*. The Jews were perfectly justified in being offended by Christ because he claimed to forgive sins.[91] It requires a remarkably high degree of spiritlessness (that is, of the order generally found in Christendom) not to be offended at some person's wanting to forgive sins if one is not a believer (and if one is, then one believes that Christ was God). And, secondly, it requires an equally remarkable spiritlessness not to be offended by the very idea that sin can be forgiven. For a human understanding that is the most impossible thing of all – not that I should extol the inability to believe it as a mark of genius, for it *shall* be believed.

Naturally, this sin was not to be found in paganism. If a pagan were able (as he was not, since he lacked the God-idea) to have the true conception of sin, he would not be able to advance beyond despairing over his sin. Indeed, what is more (and this contains all that can be conceded to human understanding and thought), one would have to commend the pagan who really managed not to despair over the world, not over himself in the usual sense, but over his sin.* That requires, humanly speaking,

* One notes therefore that despair over sin is understood dialectically in the direction of faith. That there is this dialectical aspect (even if this work only treats despair as a sickness) must never be forgotten; it is implicit in despair's being also the first element in faith. But when the direction is away from faith, from the God-relationship, then despair over sin is the new sin. In the life of spirit everything is dialectical. For indeed, as annulled possibility offence is an element in faith. But offence in the direction away from faith is sin. One can

both penetration of mind and ethical qualifications. Further than that no man as such can come, and it is rare enough for one to come this far. But Christianly everything is changed, for thou shalt believe in the forgiveness of sins.

And where is Christendom placed with respect to the forgiveness of sins? Well, the real situation of Christendom is despair of the forgiveness of sins. But this has to be grasped in the sense that Christendom is so far behind that its situation is not even apparent to it. People have not even arrived at the consciousness of sin, the only sins they know are the kind which paganism also knew, and they live on happily and contented in pagan security. But because they live in Christendom, people go further than paganism, they go on to imagine that this security is – yes, it cannot be otherwise in Christendom – that it is consciousness of the forgiveness of sins, a belief which receives every encouragement from the priest.

What has gone basically wrong with Christendom is really Christianity, that by being preached day in and day out, the doctrine of the God-man (safeguarded in the Christian understanding, be it noted, by the paradox and the possibility of offence) is taken in vain, that the difference in kind between God and man is pantheistically revoked (first with an air of superiority in speculative philosophy, then vulgarly in the streets and alley-ways).[92] Never on earth has any teaching really brought God and man so close to one another as Christianity; nor could any other: only God himself can do that, every human invention remains only a dream, an uncertain conceit. But neither has any teaching ever guarded itself so fastidiously against that most appalling of all blasphemies, that this step, once taken by God, should be taken in vain, as though God and man went together just the same – never has any teaching protected itself against this as Christianity has done, protecting

---

hold it against a person that he can never be offended by Christianity. In talking in this way, one speaks of being offended as though it were something good. And still one must say that to be offended is sin.

itself by means of the offence. Woe to the loose-talkers, woe to the loose-thinkers, and woe, woe to all that following which has learned from and praised them.

If order is to be maintained in existence – and that, after all, is what God wants, for he is not a God of confusion – then the first consideration must be that every human being is an individual human being, becomes conscious of himself as an individual human being. Once people are allowed to merge in what Aristotle terms the animal category[93] – the crowd, then this abstraction (instead of being less than nothing, less than the least significant individual human being) becomes regarded as some thing. And then it isn't long before this abstraction becomes God.[94] And then – then, *philosophice*, the doctrine of the God-man comes true. Just as in the commonwealths we learn how the crowd overawes the king, and the newspapers the privy counsellors, so at last it is discovered that the *summa summarum* of all people overawes God. This is then called the doctrine of the God-man, or the teaching that God and man are *idem per idem* [the same]. Understandably, many of the philosophers who were involved in propagating this doctrine of the superiority of the generation over the individual turn away in disgust when their teaching has sunk to the level where the mob is the God-man. But these philosophers forget that this nevertheless is their teaching, that it was not more true when accepted in the best circles, when the élite of the best circles, or a select circle of philosophers, was the incarnation.

In other words, the doctrine of the God-man has made Christendom brazen. It seems almost as if God has been too weak; as if the same had happened to him as to the good-natured man who makes too great concessions and is then rewarded with ingratitude. It is God who discovered the doctrine of the God-man, and now Christendom has cheekily turned it around and foists the kinship on God, so that God's concession amounts more or less to what it means in these times for a king to grant a more liberal constitution – and we know well enough what that means: 'He pretty well had to'. That is, it

151

is as though God had come into an embarrassing situation, as though the sensible man would be right were he to say to God: 'It's your own fault; why did you get so involved with man? It would never have occurred to any man, it would never have arisen in any man's heart,[95] that there should be this likeness between God and man. It was you yourself who had this put about, and now you are reaping the harvest.'

But Christianity has protected itself from the beginning. It begins with the doctrine of sin. The category of sin is the category of paricularity. Sin cannot at all be thought speculatively; the particular human lies below the level of the concept: one cannot think an individual human being, but only the concept 'man'. That is why speculative philosophy promptly alludes to the doctrine of the generation's *superiority* over the individual; for one cannot expect speculation to acknowledge the concept's *powerlessness* in relation to actuality. But just as one cannot 'think' a particular human being, so neither can one think a particular sinner; it is possible to think sin (then it becomes a negation), but not a particular sinner. Yet, for that very reason, there can be no seriousness with sin – when it is only to be thought. For seriousness is precisely that you and I are sinners. Seriousness is not sin in general; the accent of seriousness lies on the sinner. As for 'the particular human being', speculative philosophy, to be consistent, ought really to deal very slightingly with being a particular human being, with being something which cannot be thought. To do anything in that direction, it would have to say to the individual: 'Is this anything to waste time on? Try to forget it. To be a particular human being is to be nothing; just think – and then you are the whole of humanity, *cogito ergo sum*.'[96] Might not that possibly be a lie, and in fact the highest be the particular human being and being that particular human? Be that as it may, to be quite consistent speculative philosophy would also have to say: 'Being a particular sinner, that isn't to be anything, it falls beneath the concept; don't waste time on it', etc. And then what? Is one supposed perhaps to think sin instead of being a particular sinner (as one is required to think the concept 'man', instead of being a particular human being)? And then what? By thinking sin does a person himself perhaps become 'sin' – *cogito ergo sum*? A splendid suggestion! However, there need be no fear of becoming sin in this way – pure sin – precisely because sin cannot be thought. Even speculative philosophy would have to admit that, since sin in effect falls below the level of the concept. But, not to prolong this discussion *e concessis* [on the basis of granting something for the sake of argument], the main difficulty is something else. Speculative philosophy pays no heed to the fact that sin involves the ethical, which always points in the other direction from speculation and takes directly opposite steps; for the ethical does not abstract from actuality, but absorbs itself in it, operating essentially by means of the speculatively neglected and scorned category of the individual. Sin is a specification of the individual; it is frivolous and a new sin to pretend that being an individual sinner is nothing – when one is oneself that individual sinner. Here Christianity comes into its own; it makes the sign of the cross on speculation. It is as impossible for speculation to extricate itself from this difficulty as it is for a sailing ship to sail straight into the wind. The seriousness of sin is its actuality in the individual, whether you or me. The dialectic of sin is in direct opposition to that of speculation.

Here begins Christianity, with the doctrine of sin, and thereby with the individual.* For it is true that it is Christianity that has

* The doctrine of the sin of the race has often been abused through failure to realize that sin, however common to all, does not gather men together into a common concept, into an association or partnership ('no more than out in the graveyard [*Kirkegaarden*] the multitude of the dead form a society' [a reference to one of Kierkegaard's own works]), but splits people up into individuals and fastens hold of every individual as a sinner, a splitting up which in another sense both corresponds with and is teleologically directed towards the perfection of existence. People have been unaware of this and have therefore let the fallen race be made good again once and for all through Christ. And so, once again, God has been saddled with an abstraction which wants, as an abstraction, to claim closer kinship with him. But this is a camouflage that only makes people lose their shame. For when 'the single

taught us about the God-man, about the likeness between God
and man, but it is a great hater of flippant or impudent effrontery. Through the doctrine of sin and the particular sins, God and
Christ have once and for all made themselves safe – in quite
another way than any king – against the populace and people,
and the crowd, the public, etc.; likewise against every demand
for a more liberal constitution. All these abstractions just do not
exist for God; for God in Christ there live only particular human
beings (sinners) – and still God can encompass it all; he can take
care of the sparrows into the bargain.[97] Altogether, God is a
friend of order; and to that end he is himself present at every
point; every instant he is omnipresent (which is listed in the text
books among God's titles, and which people reflect upon a little
now and then, but never try to bear in mind every instant). His
concept is not like man's, beneath which the particular lies as
that which is incommensurable with the concept. His concept
comprises everything, and in another sense he has no concept.
God does not avail himself of an abbreviation, he grasps (*compre-
hendit*) actuality itself, all its particulars; for him the single
individual does not lie below the concept.

The doctrine of sin, the doctrine that you and I are sinners,
which doctrine unconditionally splits up 'the crowd', confirms
the qualitative difference between God and man more radically
than ever before – for once again this is something only God can

individual' feels himself akin to God (and this is what Christianity teaches),
then he also feels all the pressure of this in fear and trembling; he must
discover – as if this were not an ancient discovery – the possibility of offence.
But if the individual is to attain this glory through an abstraction, then the
whole thing becomes very easy and is really taken in vain. The single
individual does not then acquire that enormous pressure of God, which in
humbleness weighs one down as much as it uplifts; the single individual
imagines he has everything as a matter of course, merely by participating in
this abstraction. But being a man is not like being an animal, where the
specimen is always less than the species. Man is distinguished from other
animal species not just by the advantages usually mentioned, but qualitatively by the individual's, the particular individual's being more than the
species. And this specification is in turn dialectical; it means that the individual is a sinner, but then again, that it is perfection to be the individual.

do; sin is after all *before God*, etc. There is nothing in which man differs more from God than that he, and that means every human being, is a sinner, and is that 'before God', whereby the opposites are kept together in a double sense: they are held together (*continentur*), not being allowed to separate; but by being held together in this way the differences are all the more sharply apparent, just as when colours are held together *opposita juxta se posita magis illucescunt* [opposites shine more clearly in juxtaposition]. Sin is the only one of the attributes ordinarily ascribed to a human being which can in no way be said of God, either *via negationis* [by denial] or *via eminentiae* [ideally].[98] To say of God that he is not a sinner (as one says that he is not finite and is therefore, *via negationis*, infinite) is blasphemy.

As a sinner, man is separated from God by the most yawning qualitative abyss. And God is, of course, separated from man in turn by the same yawning qualitative abyss when he forgives sins. If by some inverted accommodation[99] it were possible to shift the divine over to the human, there would be one thing in which man will never come to resemble God: in the forgiveness of sins.

Here then lies the most extreme concentration of offence, something found necessary by the very doctrine that taught the likeness between God and man.

But offence is the most crucial possible specification of subjectivity, the particular human being. Clearly, thinking of offence without thinking of someone who is offended is as much an impossibility as flute-playing without a flautist.[100] But even thought has to grant that offence is, even more so than love, an intangible concept that does not take shape until there is someone, an individual, who is offended.

Offence relates, therefore, to the individual. And with this Christianity begins, by making every human being into an individual, an individual sinner. And now it focuses everything it can track down in heaven and on earth in the way of possibility of offence (and only God disposes of that): and this is

Christianity. Then it says to each individual: 'Thou shalt believe', that is, either you shall be offended, or you shall believe. Not one word more; there is nothing more to add. 'Now I have spoken', says God in heaven, 'we shall talk it over again in eternity. In the meantime you can do what you want, but judgement is at hand.'

A judgement! Indeed, we men have learned, by experience itself, that when there is a mutiny on a ship or in an army, then the guilty are so numerous that the punishment has to be dropped; and when it is the public, the highly esteemed and cultivated public, or the people, then there is not only no crime, but according to the newspaper, which is as dependable as the Gospels and the Revelation, it is God's will. Why is this so? The reason is that the concept 'judgement' corresponds to the individual; judgement cannot be passed *en masse*; people can be killed *en masse*, sprayed *en masse*, flattered *en masse*, in short can be treated in many ways just like cattle, but to judge people like cattle is not possible, for one cannot pass judgement on cattle. However many are judged, if there is to be any seriousness or truth in the judgement, then judgement is passed on each individual.* Now when the guilty are so many, it is not humanly possible to do that – which is why the whole thing is abandoned. One sees that there can be no question of any judgement, there are too many to be judged. It is impossible to get hold of them, or to get hold of them individually, so one has to give up *judging*.

And when now in our enlightened age, where all anthropomorphic and anthropopathic conceptions of God are deemed inappropriate, it is none the less not considered inappropriate to think of God as a judge, like an ordinary magistrate or a superior military judge who cannot keep track of such a wide-ranging case – then one concludes that this is just how it will be in eternity. Therefore, let us just stick together, make sure that this is what the priests preach. And if there should be an individual

---

* Note that this is why God is 'the judge'; for him there is no crowd, only particular individuals.

who dared to speak differently, an individual who was stupid enough to make his life one of concern and responsibility in fear and trembling, and on top of that wanted to make himself a nuisance to others – then let us protect ourselves by regarding him as mad or, if necessary, by putting him to death. If only there are enough of us in this, then there is no wrong in it. It is nonsense and an antiquated notion that the many can do wrong. What the many do is God's will. Before this wisdom – and we know it by experience, for we are not inexperienced youngsters, we do not speak unadvisedly, but as men of experience – before this wisdom all people have to this day bowed down – kings, emperors, and excellencies. Up to now all our cattle have received encouragement through this wisdom. So, God is damned well going to learn to bow down too. It is simply a matter of there being many of us, a decent number, who stick together; if we do that we are made safe against the judgement of eternity. They are indeed made safe, if it is only in eternity that they are to become individuals. But they were, and are, constantly individuals before God. The man sitting in a glass case is not so constrained as is each human being in his transparency before God. This is the way it is with conscience. Things are so arranged, by means of conscience, that the report follows immediately upon each guilt, and that the guilty person is the one who has to write it. But it is written with invisible ink, and only becomes properly legible when held up to the light in eternity while eternity does its audit of the consciences. Essentially, everyone arrives at eternity bringing with him the most exact record of every least trifle he has committed or omitted to hand over. In eternity, therefore, passing judgement is something even a child could manage; really there is nothing for a third party to do, everything down to the most insignificant word passed is in order. For the guilty person *en route* through life to eternity, it is like the murderer who fled the scene of his crime – and his crime – with all speed by rail; alas!, just below the carriage in which he sat ran the electro-magnetic telegraph with his description and orders to apprehend him at the first station. When he came to the station and climbed down from the carriage he was arrested. In a way, he had brought his own indictment with him.

And so despair of the forgiveness of sins is offence. And offence is the intensification of sin. This is something people generally never consider; generally they would hardly reckon offence to be a sin, of which in any case they do not speak, but of sins, among which there is no place for offence. That is because they do not make the opposition, Christianly, between sin and faith, but between sin and virtue.

C

The sin of abandoning Christianity modo ponendo [positively], *of declaring it to be untruth*

This is sin against the Holy Spirit. Here the self is at the height of despair: it not only throws all of Christianity aside, but makes it out to be lies and falsehood – what a stupendously despairing conception such a self must have of itself!

The intensification of sin is clearly visible when grasped as a war between man and God where the tactics change; the intensification is an escalation from the defensive to the offensive. Sin is despair; here the fight is carried on evasively. Then came despair over sin; here the fight is again carried on evasively or through retrenchment of the position of withdrawal, though constantly *pedem referens* [in retreat]. Now the tactics are altered; although sin becomes more and more absorbed in itself and so withdraws, in a sense it nevertheless comes closer, becomes more and more decisively itself. Despair of the forgiveness of sins is a definite position directly opposed to an offer of God's compassion; sin is now not wholly in retreat, not merely defensive. But the sin of abandoning Christianity as a falsehood and a lie is offensive warfare. In a way, all the previous forms of despair conceded superior strength to the opponent; but now sin is the aggressor.

Sin against the Holy Ghost is the positive form of being offended.[101]

Christianity's teaching is the doctrine of the God-man, of the kinship between God and man, though in such a way, be it noted, that the possibility of offence is, if I may be so bold, the guarantee by which God makes sure that man does not come too close. The possibility of offence is the dialectical element in all that is Christian. Take it away, and Christianity becomes mere paganism, though something so fantastic that paganism would have to call it stuff and nonsense. To be as near to God as Christianity teaches that man can come to him, and dares to come to him, and in Christ is to come to him, has never occurred to any human being. Now if this is to be understood literally, just as it is and without the least little reservation, and in an altogether natural and free and easy manner, then if paganism's poetic fiction of the gods were to be called a form of human lunacy, Christianity would have to be a lunatic invention of God; only a God who had taken leave of his senses could have hit upon such a doctrine – that is how a human being still in command of his wits must judge it. The incarnate God, if one wanted to be on brotherly terms with him, would then be a counterpart of Prince Henry in Shakespeare.[102]

God and man are two qualities separated by an infinite difference in kind. Every doctrine that ignores this difference is, humanly speaking, insane; divinely understood, it is blasphemy. In paganism, man made God a man (the man-God); in Christianity God makes himself man (the God-man) – but in the infinite love of his compassionate grace he none the less makes one condition; he cannot do otherwise. Precisely this is Christ's grief: 'he cannot do otherwise'.[103] He can debase himself, take the form of a servant, suffer, die for men, invite all to come up to him,[104] offer up every day of his life and every hour of the day, and offer up his life – but the possibility of offence he cannot take away. Ah!, singular work of love. Ah!, unfathomable grief of love, that even God cannot – as in another sense neither will he, nor can he will, but even if he wanted to – cannot make it impossible for this work of love to turn into just the opposite for man, be the most utmost misery! For the greatest possible human misery, greater even than sin, is to be offended by Christ and to continue in offence. And Christ cannot, 'love' cannot, make this impossible. Does he not say, 'And blessed is he, whosoever shall not be offended in me'?[105] More he cannot do. Accordingly, by his love he can – it is possible – make a person as miserable as a person could never be otherwise. Oh! unfathomable contradiction in love! But still, in love he cannot find it in his heart not to complete this work of love; alas!, even though it makes a man more miserable than otherwise he would ever have been!

Let us speak of this in purely human terms. Oh! how pitiable a person who has never felt the loving urge to sacrifice everything for love, who has therefore been unable to do so! But then, when he found that this very sacrifice of his in love might – could possibly – cause the other person, the loved one, the greatest unhappiness, what then? Either his love would lose its buoyant vigour, its vital energy collapse into a pent-up plaintiveness, he would abandon love, not dare perform this work of love, even giving way under the weight, not of the work but of this possibility. For just as a weight becomes infinitely heavier when placed at the end of a rod where the lifter is to take hold of the opposite end, so every act becomes infinitely heavier when it becomes dialectical, and heaviest when it becomes sympathetico-dialectical, so that what love prompts one to do for the loved one looks in another sense as though intended to put the loved one off. Or the love would triumph, and he would venture to do it out of love. Ah!, but in the joy of love (as love always is joyful, especially when it sacrifices everything), there would none the less be a deep sorrow – for there was indeed that possibility! Well, then, he would complete this work of love of his, he would make the sacrifice (in which for his part he would exult), but not without tears; for above this – what shall I call it? – this historical painting of the inner life, there looms that dark possibility. And still, had it not loomed over him, his work would not have been one of true love. Oh!, my friend, what is it you have attempted in life? Tax your brain, tear off every wrapping and lay bear the viscera of feeling in your breast, demolish every fortification that separates you from the one of whom you are reading, and then read Shakespeare – you will shudder at the collisions. But the really religious collisions even Shakespeare seems to have recoiled from. Perhaps these can only be expressed in the language of the gods. And that language no man can speak; for as a Greek has already put it so beautifully: 'From men man learns to speak, from the gods to keep silent.'[106]

That there is an infinite difference in kind between God and man, that is the possibility of offence which cannot be taken away. Out of love, God becomes man. He says: 'See, here is what it is to be a human being'; but he adds: 'Take care, for I am also God – blessed is he who is not offended in me.' As man he takes the form of a lowly servant, he shows what it is to be a man of humble station so that no one should feel himself excluded or think that it is human status and respect among one's fellows that bring one closer to God. No, he is the lowly man. 'Look over here', he says, 'and learn what it is to be a human being; oh! but take care, for I am also God – blessed is he who is not offended in me.' Or conversely: 'The Father and I are one,[107] and yet I am this particular, lowly man, poor, forsaken, delivered into the hands of men – blessed is he who is not offended in me. I, this lowly man, am he who makes the deaf hear, the blind see, the lame walk, lepers clean, the dead rise up – blessed is he who is not offended in me.'[108]

Therefore, making myself accountable to the highest authority, I make so bold as to say that this phrase, 'Blessed is he who is not offended in me', is part of the preaching concerning Christ, though not in the same way as the words of institution at the Lord's supper, at least like the words, 'Let each man examine himself.'[109] They are Christ's own words and, particularly in Christendom, they must be urged again and again, repeated and addressed to each one individually. Wherever

KIERKEGAARD

these words do not resound,* at any rate where the presentation of Christianity is not permeated at every point by this thought, Christianity is blasphemy. For with no bodyguard and servants to prepare his way and call people's attention to who it was who came, Christ walked here upon earth in the form of a lowly servant. But the possibility of offence (oh! what grief it brought to him in his love!) guarded and guards him, securing a yawning abyss between him and the person who was closest to him and stood nearest.

He who is not offended *worships* in faith. But to worship, which is the expression of faith, is to show that the infinitely yawning qualitative abyss between them is secured. For in faith the possibility of offence is again the dialectical element.†

But the kind of offence here in question is *modo ponendo* [positive]; it says of Christianity that it is untruth and a lie, and therefore it says the same about Christ.

To illustrate this kind of offence, it is best to review the various forms of offence, which are primarily related to the paradox (Christ) and so recur with every specification of Christianity,

* As is now the case almost everywhere in Christendom, which apparently *either* altogether ignores the fact that it is Christ himself who so repeatedly and fervently warned against offence, even, up to the very end of his life, to his faithful apostles who had followed him from the beginning and for his sake had given up everything; *or* perhaps tacitly takes this to be an exaggerated fear on the part of Christ, seeing that experience proves thousand upon thousand times that one can believe in Christ without remarking the least possibility of offence. But this might well be a mistake which will no doubt come to light when the possibility of offence judges Christendom.

† Here is a small task for observers. If one assumes that all the many priests, here and abroad, who hold and write sermons, are believing Christians, how can it be explained that one never hears or reads the prayer which especially in our times would be so apt: 'God in heaven, I thank you for not requiring a person to comprehend Christianity, for if it were required, then I would be of all men the most miserable. The more I seek to comprehend it, the more I discover merely the possibility of offence. Therefore, I thank you for requiring only faith and I pray you will continue to increase it.' From the point of view of orthodoxy, this prayer would be altogether correct and, assuming sincerity on the part of the one who gave it, it would also be a well-directed irony on the whole of speculation. But I wonder, shall one find faith on the earth? [This contains references to I Corinthians and Luke. *Translator.*]

because every specification relates to Christ, has Christ *in mente* [in mind].

The lowest form of offence, humanly speaking the most innocent, is to leave the whole issue of Christ undecided, to pronounce in effect: 'I don't presume to judge the matter; I do not believe, but I pass no judgement.' That this is a form of offence escapes most people. The point is that they have quite forgotten this Christian, *'Thou shalt'*. That is why they fail to see that this is offence, this being neutral about Christ. The fact that Christianity is proclaimed to you means you are to make up your mind about Christ. That he is, or that he exists and that he has existed, is decisive for all existence. If Christ is proclaimed to you, then it is offence to say, 'I don't wish to have any opinion about it.'

But we must understand this with a certain reservation when Christianity is proclaimed as indifferently as it is in our time. No doubt there are many thousands alive today who have heard Christianity proclaimed and have never heard anything about this 'shall'. But for the person who has heard it, if he says: 'I don't wish to have any opinion about it', then he is offended. He is denying the divinity of Christ when he denies that it has the right to demand of such a person that he have an opinion. It does not help for such a person to say: 'I'm not saying anything, neither "yes" nor "no", about Christ,' for then one simply asks him: 'Have you no opinion, either, as to whether you *shall* have an opinion about him or not?' If he answers 'yes' to that, then he has caught himself in a trap; and if he answers 'no', then Christianity judges for him all the same, that he shall have an opinion about this, and accordingly about Christ in turn, that no man shall have the audacity to leave Christ's life in abeyance as though it were some curiosity. That God lets himself be born and becomes a human being, is no idle whim, something that occurs to him so as to have something to do, perhaps to put a stop to the boredom that has brashly been said to be bound up with being God[110] – it is not to have an adventure. No, the fact that God does this is the seriousness of existence. And the seriousness in this seriousness is, in turn, that each *shall* have an opinion about it. When a king visits a provincial town he regards it as an affront if a public servant, unless of course legitimately excused, fails to pay his respects. But how would he judge it if one were to take no notice of the fact that the king was in town, were to play the private citizen who says in this regard: 'I couldn't care less for His Majesty and the Royal Law!'[111] So, too, when it pleases God to become man – that it so pleases a man (and as a public servant is to the king, so each individual human being is to God) to say: 'Well, this is something I don't care to form any opinion about.' This is the superiority with which one talks about what one basically has no regard for – with which one disregards God.

The next form of offence is the negative, but passive, form. Certainly it feels it cannot take no notice of Christ, leaving this business of Christ in abeyance and carrying on a busy life is something it is incapable of. But believing is something it cannot do either; so it stays staring at one and the same point, at the paradox. To some extent it honours Christianity all the same in that it is an acknowledgement that this question, 'What do you think of Christ?', is really the most crucial one. A person offended in this way lives on as a shadow; his life is consumed because in his heart he is constantly concerned with this crux. And thus he is testimony (as is the pain of unhappy love in relation to love) to the reality that is Christianity's.

The final form of offence is the one we are discussing, the positive form. It declares Christianity to be untruth and a lie. It denies Christ (that he has existed and that he is the one he claimed to be) either Docetically or rationalistically,[112] so that either Christ does not become a particular human being, but only appears to do so, or he becomes *only* a particular human being. Thus, either Docetically he becomes poesy, mythology, which makes no claims on actuality, or rationalistically he becomes an actuality that makes no claim to be divine. Of course, this denial of Christ as the paradox implies in turn the denial of everything Christian: sin, the forgiveness of sins, etc.

This form of offence is sin against the Holy Ghost. As the Jews said of Christ, that he cast out devils with the help of the devil,[113] so this offence makes Christ into an invention of the devil.

This way of being offended is the highest intensification of sin, which one usually overlooks because one does not make the opposition, Christianly, between sin and faith.

On the other hand, that opposition has been effective throughout this work, which laid down straight away (Part One, A.*A* [p. 43]) the formula for that state in which there is no despair at all: in relating itself to itself and in wanting to be itself, the self is grounded transparently in the power which established it. Which formula in turn, as has frequently been remarked, is the definition of faith.

NOTES

1. *Herr! gieb uns blöde Augen für Dinge, die nichts taugen, und Augen voller Klarheit in alle deine Wahrheit.* In his manuscript (see *Søren Kierkegaards Papirer*, 20 vols., Gyldendal, Copenhagen, 1918, VIII², 171 6, p. 268) Kierkegaard gives the source as a sermon by Bishop Albertini, cf. *Handbuch deutscher Beredsamkeit* v. Dr O. L. B. Wolff, Leipzig, 1845, iste D. p. 293.

2. The original has *eller lege Forundringsleg med Verdenshistorien* (lit. to play wonder-game with world-history). The Danish dictionary (*Ordbog over det danske Sprog*, bd. 5, København, 1923) tells us that this 'wonder-game' (otherwise 'sitting on the wonder-chair') is a party game in which one person is put on a chair in the centre while another goes round the circle of participants asking them why the person in the middle (in this case world-history) is to be so admired, and then confronts the latter with these (whispered) answers so that the latter can try to guess who gave them.

3. In his first major work, *Either/Or*, published six years earlier in 1843, the only effective remedy for despair is said to be to go through with it, to *choose* despair is already in some sense to have got the better of it (see *Either/Or*, II, tr. W. Lowrie, Doubleday, New York, 1959, pp. 215 and 217).

4. The Danish *afdøe* (lit. 'die away') is commonly used in participle form in death notices in the sense of 'the departed'.

5. It may sound a little strange that the relation itself should be a unity. Normally one would regard the unity as the whole comprising the relation and the elements in the relation. There are two radically different ways of mitigating the anomaly: one can either translate *Eenhed* as 'unit' rather than 'unity', letting the relation have the status of a third element or 'term', or else interpret Kierkegaard's 'relation' in an active sense as 'that in

which the unity of the elements or terms consists'. This seems to be the correct alternative. One can then distinguish a 'negative' unity, where the activity is so to speak merely latent and the (here) two constituent terms interact on their own, the relation as it were only providing the path along which the interactions occur. A 'positive' unity, however, is one in which the unity is actually supervised by the relation, which then in a sense *is* the whole in which the constituents are contained. The latter alternative conforms with Kierkegaard's usage elsewhere (see *The Concept of Dread*, also translated 'The Concept of Anxiety'), and is therefore the recommended one. My own interpolation of 'term' here after 'third', in the interests of idiomatic English, may make things look more anomalous than they are.

6. Here, as frequently in this work, Kierkegaard uses the expression *under Bestemmelsen*, meaning 'under the qualification (of)'. I have translated it sometimes, as here, as 'from the point of view (of)', and at other times as 'under the aspect [or category] (of)'. Both capture the force of the original while freeing the translation of a terminology that might otherwise appear unnecessarily dated.

7. The Danish *Misforhold* neatly contrasts with the notion of the relation (*Forhold*) in which the lack of proportion or balance is to be found. But the English 'misrelation' does not have this primary sense, and in any case the surface contrast can suggest misleadingly that the 'misrelationship' amounts to an absence of relationship, rather than, as Kierkegaard here emphasizes, to a mode of the relationship. The mode, or modes, of imbalance or disproportion in question might also be called 'disorder', 'discrepancy', 'discord', 'disparity', and so on, i.e. ways in which the terms in the relation do not 'harmonize' or 'get on' with one another, or do not modify one another.

8. The most idiomatic translation of the Danish *Virkelighed* would perhaps be 'reality', but Kierkegaard uses the term in the sense, derived from Aristotle, of a realization of an inherent possibility. 'Actuality' conveys this better. Moreover, Kierkegaard uses *Realitet* (here translated 'reality') to mean something like 'of practical consequence' or 'genuinely existing', marking a distinction not with possibility, but with having a merely abstract status and the like.

9. Kierkegaard's editors plausibly take this to be a reference to the earlier *Philosophical Fragments* (1844) under the philosophical pseudonym 'Johannes Climacus', particularly the section entitled 'Interlude'.

10. In *Søren Kierkegaards Papirer* (VIII², 145 3, p. 244) there is a note Kierkegaard made in the margin here attributing the line to 'a poem by Ewald on suicide'.

11. Mark 9.47–8. 'And if thine eye offend thee, pluck it out: it is better for thee to enter the kingdom of God with one eye, than having two eyes, to be cast into hell fire: where their worm dieth not, and the fire is not quenched.'

12. Kierkegaard's words, *det Hidsende* and *den kolde Brand*, can suggest the physical states of inflammation and mortification (or gangrene or necrosis [*Koldbrand*]), metaphors which cohere nicely with his descriptions, just below, of despair as internal gnawing and of an increase in despair as a rising fever.

13. Caesar Borgia's motto: *Aut Caesar aut nihil*.

14. In Plato's *Republic*, X, 608ff.

15. The translation may seem a trifle heavy-handed here. Kierkegaard indulges in a little word-play some lines later with the words *Lykke*, ordinarily translated 'happiness', and *lykkes*, meaning 'succeed'. In Danish this would not be to pun, since the words have related meanings. *Lykke* means 'happiness' in the sense of the pleasurable state of mind attendant upon success or good fortune, but it can also mean more emphatically good fortune itself, as is also implicit in the English word ('hap' as 'good luck', and 'to hap' as 'to happen by chance'). The verb form *lykkes* (to succeed; and *mislykkes*, to fail) also carries the sense of 'having the good luck or fortune to succeed' or 'having the bad luck or fortune to fail'. It is an important theme in Kierkegaard's writings that a life based on a reliance on good or bad fortune is a life without a self, without spirit. It is a life of 'immediacy' (see below), vulnerable to fate, and the 'womanly youthfulness' discussed here is a personification of the 'fortunate felicity' that belongs (transiently) to immediacy. Because of the centrality of the notion, I have translated as 'good fortune' what would be translated more smoothly as 'happiness'. Usually, where the word 'happiness' (etc.) appears in this

translation, it is a rendering of what in Danish would also clearly convey the idea of good fortune.

16. The context, as here, often calls for 'happiness' rather than 'good fortune'.

17. In fact Kierkegaard's text only has *Lykke* here.

18. The original has *paa, hvorledes Dette reflekterer sig*, or 'on how the latter reflects himself'.

19. Fichte saw in the 'productive power of the imagination' the source of our concept of the external world (the *Not-I*) and so also of the basic categories of thought. See J. G. Fichte, *Grundriss des Eigenthümlichen der Wissenschaftslehre, Sämmtliche Werke*, I – XI, Berlin and Bonn, 1834–46, I, 1, pp. 386–7.

20. The bands had sixty members, each with an instrument that could play only one note which was inserted at the appropriate places. Kierkegaard mistakenly writes 'bar' (*Takt*) for 'note'.

21. Luke 10.41–2. 'And Jesus answered, and said unto her, "Martha, Martha, thou art careful, and troubled about many things: but one thing is needful, and Mary hath chosen that good part, which shall not be taken away from her".'

22. In a marginal note (see *Søren Kierkegaards Papirer*, VIII[2], B 150 7, p. 247) Kierkegaard writes: 'If fantasized lives [*de phantastiske Existentser*] may be said to pawn themselves to the devil, then the narrow-minded despairers pawn themselves to the world ... They have eyes for what lies outside, but are inwardly blind; their relation to a spiritual person is like that of a statue to someone living; they are human beings only in appearance, like the elves (*Elverpigerne*) who are hollow at the back.' The latter is a reference to fleeting figures in folklore – e.g., beautiful young maidens – with hollowed-out backs ('like a kneading trough') who might vanish if they were asked to turn around to show they were as full-bodied from behind as they were from in front.

23. Απειρον (*apeiron*) means 'unlimited', in a philosophical context particularly in the sense of lacking any distinct quality or means of differentiation, i.e. indeterminateness. It is connected with the idea of infinitude through the idea of lack of limit or of boundary conveyed by the latter. As soon as one attaches a description to something, that thing is 'defined', or 'delimited' in the sense that it is set conceptually apart from anything that

does not answer to that description. Πέρας (*peras*) means 'limit'. The distinction is originally due to the pre-Socratic thinker Anaximander, and is central, e.g., in Plato's *Philebus*, where it is used to make a distinction, closer perhaps to Kierkegaard's intention, between the mere content of a certain way of life and some guiding principle which gives the content the form of a good life.

24. See, e.g., Hegel's *Logic* (tr. William Wallace, Clarendon Press, Oxford, 1975, p. 208): 'Necessity has been defined, and rightly so, as the union of possibility and actuality.'

25. Kierkegaard, who did not read English, quotes Friedrich von Schlegel's German translation. Schlegel was the leader of the German Romantic movement and some of the themes of his thought are taken up by Kierkegaard, e.g., irony as a liberating attitude (cf. Kierkegaard's doctoral dissertation, *The Concept of Irony*) and genius (cf. *The Concept of Dread*).

26. This corresponds to the notion of faith illustrated by the story of Abraham's willingness to sacrifice Isaac in *Fear and Trembling* (tr. Alastair Hannay, Penguin, Harmondsworth, 1985).

27. As a mark of his gratitude for kind treatment, Silenus (the constant companion of Dionysus) allowed King Midas to ask him a favour. King Midas requested that everything he touched be turned to gold. The request was granted, but since even the food he touched became gold, he asked the god to take back the favour. Dionysus thereupon ordered him to bathe in the sources of the Pactolus near Mt Tmolus. Midas was saved, and the sand in a river-bed was thereafter rich in gold. (See *A Smaller Classical Dictionary*, J. M. Dent & Sons, London, 1937.)

28. Appropriately here, the Danish for 'breathing in' (*inaande*) and 'breathing out' (*udaande*), like the English 'aspiration' (or 'inspiration') and 'expiration', includes the word for spirit (*Aand*).

29. Kierkegaard's rendering of Spinoza's *veritas norma sui et falsi est* (note to *Ethics* Pt. II, Prop. XLIII: 'He who has a true idea, knows at the same time that he has a true idea, nor can he doubt concerning the truth of things.' The same note contains the well-known saying, 'Truth is its own standard.')

30. The phrase points to the contrast between 'spirit' in Hegel's world-historical sense, in which individuals merely participate, and in terms of which Absolute Spirit is an ideal projected into

an indefinite future, and 'spirit' in Kierkegaard's individualistic sense, according to which every person potentially is and both can and should become spirit.

31. Kierkegaard is referring to Hegel and his 'System' of philosophy. See n. 70.

32. A reference to Kierkegaard's earlier book on themes related closely to those of this one. *The Concept of Dread* (1844) contains a section entitled 'Spiritlessness's dread'.

33. See the translator's Introduction.

34. See Grimm, *Irische Elfenmärchen*, Leipzig, 1826, p. lxxxiii.

35. In his later campaign against the Church (see the translator's Introduction) Kierkegaard refers disparagingly to the institutionalized Christianity of his time as *Christenheden*, translated 'Christendom', while Kierkegaard's term *Christendommen* is translated 'Christianity'.

36. This is the theme of Kierkegaard's *Works of Love* (1847).

37. Cf. Augustine, *The City of God*, XIX, 25.

38. The Danish for suicide is *Selvmord* (self-murder).

39. A figure of speech or any arrangement of items in which what logically, naturally, or (as here) chronologically, comes last is put first.

40. That is, as in the earlier section on the forms of despair, in the actual conditions which constrain its possiblity in the sense of providing the context (of the concrete self) in which possibilities are to be actualized.

41. Goethe, *Faust* (tr. B. Taylor, Euphorion Books, London, n.d.), Pt. I, Scene 4: 'Take hold, then! let reflection rest, And plunge into the world with zest! I say to thee, a speculative wight Is like a beast on moorlands lean, That round and round some fiend misleads to evil plight, While all about lie pastures fresh and green' (Mephistopheles to Faust, p. 73).

42. From Virgil's *Aeneid*, II, 325 (*The Aeneid of Virgil* I–II, tr. C. Day Lewis, Hogarth Press, London 1954: 'We Trojans, with Ilium and all its Teucrian glory, Are things of the past' (I, p. 40).

43. The word *Indesluttedhed* is part of everyday Danish and used to refer to a normal kind of reticence or reserve. But its literal translation, 'enclosedness' (or 'pent-inness' or 'pent-upness') expresses the defensive aspect of reserve rather better than the English term (which is perhaps over-associated with a certain

kind of cultivated lack of expressiveness), and is therefore also better adapted to expressing the states in the negative development described by Kierkegaard. But since in Danish it is a perfectly ordinary word that refers to a quite common character trait, I have preferred 'reserve' ('being reserved', etc.) as the translation.

44. In Shakespeare's *Richard III*, Act 4, Scene 4, Richard has drums beaten to drown his mother's curses: 'A flourish, trumpets! Strike alarum, drums! Let not the hearers hear these tell-tale women Rail on the Lord's anointed: Strike, I say!'

45. Genesis 1.1: 'In the beginning God created heaven and earth.'

46. Matthew 16.19: 'And I will give unto thee the keys of the kingdom of heaven: and whatsoever thou shalt bind on earth, shall be bound in heaven: and whatsoever thou shalt loose on earth, shall be loosed in heaven.'

47. Prometheus was nailed (or chained) to a rock by Zeus on Mt Caucasus where during the day eagles consumed his liver, which was restored during the night.

48. Kierkegaard's term is *Servitut*. In civil law a 'Servitude' is a prescriptive inconvenience (e.g., a thoroughfare) to which real property may be liable.

49. Kierkegaard's *Bibehold* or 'retention' is a legal term concerned with rights of ownership.

50. Kierkegaard's term for direct defiance of what is recognized to be good. In referring a little later to a 'purely Greek sense', he distinguishes his own from a morally neutral use (δαίμων [daemon] – an intermediate and morally neutral being between gods and men).

51. Kierkegaard here plays on the contrast between *Indelukke* (an enclosure) and *Udelukkende* (exclusively), both comparable with *Indesluttethed* (reserve). Reserve consists here in the despair's making an enclosure exclusively for itself.

52. The reference and the whole passage that follows are clearly autobiographical. In his marginal notes (*Søren Kierkegaards Papirer*, VIII^2, B 158, p. 253) Kierkegaard describes this poet-existence in terms of the form of reserved despair in which a person, because he despairs over something earthly and then over his weakness in not being capable of attaining whatever it was, is really despairing of the eternal in himself. His attachment

to the earthly is a despairing attempt to locate the eternal aspect in something finite. But really there is a deep religious need, and the idea of God is something the despairer takes with him into his reserve as 'the fresh-water spring inside its mountain stronghold . . .'

53. Nürnberg, once a centre of medieval painting and the birthplace of Dürer, later became famous for its cheap-art industry, the products of which were peddled around Europe.

54. The 'earlier' dogmatics are to be found in the sixteenth-century *Augsburg Confession*, the so-called 'Augustana' (Apologia Confessionis Augustanae, see Art. II, sects. 7ff.), which defines the difference between the Lutheran and the Catholic faith. It was a Lutheran orthodoxy that the guilt of sin, being infinite since it offends the infinite majesty of God, deserves infinite punishment. The 'later' dogmatics (as the editors of the Danish edition mention) could be a reference to denials (e.g., in Immanuel Kant) that the moral law is determined by God's will, a denial which removes the importance of the idea of one's sin being 'before God'.

55. Ephesians 2.11–12: 'Wherefore remember that ye *being* in past time Gentiles . . . at that time ye were without Christ . . .'

56. Pelagius (*c.*360–*c.*431) was a British monk who denied the Catholic doctrine of original sin. He taught that man could achieve salvation and the good life without the special help or grace of God.

57. A clear reference to the period following Kierkegaard's breach with his father (see the translator's Introduction).

58. Matthew 12.24: 'but when the Pharisees heard it, they said, This *fellow* doth not cast out devils, but by Beelzebub the prince of the devils'.

59. The 'paradox' that God, who is eternal (i.e. timeless), came into being, lived and died (timed events), and also that God the eternal took on the form of the least significant of men. The concept is central to earlier works of Kierkegaard, notably *Philosophical Fragments* (1844) and *Concluding Unscientific Postscript to the Philosophical Fragments* (1846). It implies that Christianity is based on a conceptually unintelligible premise. Actually being before God is intellectually absurd. See the translator's Introduction (p. 12).

60. I Corinthians 2.9: 'But as it is written, Eye hath not seen, nor ear heard, neither have entered in the heart of man, the things which God hath prepared for them that love him.'

61. Ballad-wives (*Visekjerlinger* or *Visekællinger*) functioned as disseminators of contemporary scandals by offering for sale (and sometimes singing in notoriously raucous voices) ballads minted for the occasion.

62. 'The market-town' (*Kjøbstaden* – now *Købstaden*) is a disparaging allusion to Copenhagen (*Kjøbenhavn* – now *København* – lit. market-harbour), a town of some size (with a population at the time of about 127,000). In *The Point of View for My Work as an Author* (published posthumously in 1859) Kierkegaard lamented his fate as a 'genius in a market-town'.

63. For Aristotle (*Nicomachean Ethics*) moral virtue involves following a mean course (the 'golden mean') between extremes (which are the vices). Thus courage is a mean between foolhardiness and cowardice. Cf. also Horace, *Odes*, II, x, 5.

64. The 'categorical imperative' is the basis of Immanuel Kant's ethical theory. It is an imperative that is not conditional upon some given choice of goal. Kant meant that people act ethically, or morally, only when they accept that the rule of behaviour (the maxim) to which their action corresponds is applicable equally to anyone in the same situation. In saying that the Greeks posited an intellectual categorical imperative, Kierkegaard implies that they assumed moral conduct emerged spontaneously from the understanding.

65. Kierkegaard's actual words translate as 'dressed in Adrienne'. The allusion is to Ludvig Holberg's comedy, *Den politiske kandstøber* (The Armchair Politician), 1.2, and IV.2. An Adrienne (or Adriane) was a fancy gown, fastened above but open at the front and with a train. In the play a servant describes how his master tried unsuccessfully to get his 'god-fearing, old-fashioned' wife to go out in an 'Adriane', and later dons one himself to everyone's amazement. The idea is that the attire is not the man.

66. Cf. Philippians 2.7: 'but made himself of no reputation, and took upon himself the form of a servant, and was made in the likeness of men'.

67. Matthew 27.30, and Luke 18.32: 'For he shall be delivered unto

the Gentiles, and shall be mocked, and spitefully entreated, and spitted on.'

68. Kierkegaard is no doubt alluding to the Primate of Denmark, Bishop J. P. Mynster, a strong influence on Kierkegaard in his youth, but whom Kierkegaard bitterly attacked in later years as a symbol of all that was wrong with 'Christendom'.

69. Sound-image (*Klangfigur*) or the so-called Chladni figure (after its discoverer, the German acoustician, E. F. F. Chladni, 1756 –1827), which occurs on, e.g., a glass plate covered lightly with sand and held at one point, when sounded with a violin bow.

70. Hegel's *Phenomenology of Spirit* (1807) is described on its title page as the first part of a 'System of Science' to be completed in later works. The 'system', later rebegun, included *Science of Logic, Philosophy of Nature* and *Philosophy of Mind*. It was intended as an all-embracing science of human life as 'absolute spirit'.

71. The one indubitable truth which formed the basis of Descartes's account of human scientific knowledge.

72. Cf. Matthew 9.29: 'Then touched he their eyes, saying, "According to your faith, be it unto you".'

73. Kierkegaard's heading reads, 'That sin is not a negation but a position.' The terms are philosophical, a 'position' being something 'posited', laid down as a fact, positively affirmed, and not reducible to anything more basic.

74. This is generally taken to be a reference to Professor H. L. Martensen, who had earlier been Kierkegaard's university tutor, and whose *Den christelige Dogmatik* appeared in the same year as *The Sickness unto Death*.

75. Hegelian philosophy was offered as a 'science' of human spirit. See n. 70.

76. Expressions from Spinoza's *Ethics*.

77. Psalms 61.10.

78. This was what the Delphic oracle said about Socrates (Plato, *Apology*, 20 d–21).

79. See n. 70.

80. Galatians 3.22: 'But the scripture hath concluded all under sin, that the promise by faith of Jesus Christ might be given to them that believe.'

81. See page 128.

82. Revelation 3.16: 'So then because thou art lukewarm, and neither cold nor hot, I will spew thee out of my mouth.'

83. Romans 14.23: 'And he that doubteth, is damned if he eat, because he eateth not of faith: for whatever is not of faith, is sin.'

84. Matthew 7.13–14: 'Enter ye in at the strait gate, for wide is the gate, and broad is the way that leadeth to destruction, and many there be which go in thereat: because strait is the gate, and narrow is the way which leadeth unto life, and few there be that find it.'

85. Kierkegaard, who read Shakespeare only in Schlegel and Tieck's German translation, quotes as always the German which in fact here suits the context better than the original, and retranslates into English as, 'Works sprung from sin acquire only through sin their strength and power.'

86. Part I, Scene 14 ('Forest and Cavern'). In Taylor's translation (see n. 41): 'Naught so insipid in the world I find / As is a devil in despair' (p. 112).

87. In this case the German translation by Schlegel and Tieck quoted by Kierkegaard is a close rendering of the original.

88. Fate, Providence and Governance are different and progressively less 'alienated' ways in which Kierkegaard conceives the individual's relation to its own finite destiny.

89. The passage plays upon the Danish term for insolence, impudence, effrontery (*Nærgaaenhed*) which is literally translated 'going nearness'. The notions of ef-frontery and bare-facedness allow a similar, though less graphic, play of words in English.

90. A reference to Kant's ethical theory according to which 'ought' implies 'can'. That is, what the categorical imperative (see n. 64) enjoins is always something it is within the agent's power to accomplish.

91. Matthew 9.2–3, Mark 2.7. The scribes regarded as blasphemy Christ's forgiveness (on 'seeing their faith') of the sins of those stricken with palsy.

92. The former refers to Hegel's speculative idealism, the latter to the materialist inversion of Hegel's understanding of Christianity in the writings of Ludwig A. Feuerbach (e.g., in *The Essence of Christianity*, 1841).

93. See Aristotle, *Politics*, III, 11.

94. Very likely a reference to David F. Strauss, whose two-volume

The Life of Jesus Critically Examined (translated, as in the case of Feuerbach's book, by George Eliot) had appeared in 1835–6. Strauss became a popular exponent of the view that Christianity was an expression of the human mind's capacity to generate myths and treat them as truths revealed by God to man. In a later work (*The Christian Theory of Belief,* 1840–41) he saw Christianity, with its doctrine of the God-man, as a development towards a true pantheism, thus eliminating the 'qualitative difference' between the two conjuncts.

95. I Corinthians 2.9: 'But as it is written, Eye hath not seen, nor ear heard, neither have entered into the heart of man, the things which God hath prepared for them that love him.' Kierkegaard recurs frequently (e.g., the final page of *Philosophical Fragments*) to the thought that Christianity could never have occurred to a human mind.

96. See n. 70.

97. Matthew 10.29: 'Are not two sparrows sold for a farthing? and one of them shall not fall on the ground without your Father.'

98. The *via negationis* defines God, saying what finite imperfections God does not have, the *via eminentiae* by affirming what positive characteristics God has in their perfect forms.

99. 'Accommodation' is Enlightenment theology's term for the adaptation of the divine revelation to human limitations. The human limitations thus determine the revealed nature of the divine.

100. See Plato, *Apology*, 27 b.

101. Matthew 12.32–3: 'Wherefore I say unto you, All manner of sin and blasphemy shall be forgiven unto men: but the blasphemy against the Holy Ghost shall not be forgiven unto men. And whosoever speaketh a word against the Son of man, it shall be forgiven him: but whosoever speaketh against the Holy Ghost, it shall not be forgiven him, neither in this world, neither in the world to come.' Cf. Mark 3.29; Luke 12.10.

102. In *King Henry IV*, the Prince of Wales, later to become Henry V, appears as a boon companion of Falstaff.

103. Martin Luther's final word at the Diet of Worms.

104. Matthew 11.28: 'Come unto me all ye that labour, and are heavy laden, and I will give you rest.'

105. Matthew 11.6.

106. Plutarch, 'De garrulitate', 8, *Moralia*, 506 a: 'in speaking we have men as teachers, but in keeping silent we have gods, and we receive from them this lesson of silence at initiations into the Mysteries' (*Plutarch's Moralia*, tr. F. C. Babbitt *et al.*, Heinemann, London, 1927–67, VI, p. 417).
107. John 10.30; 17.21.
108. Matthew 11.5–6: 'the blind receive their sight, and the lame walk, the lepers are cleansed, and the deaf hear, the dead are raised up, and the poor have the gospel preached to them. And blessed is he, whosoever shall not be offended in me.'
109. I Corinthians 11.28: 'But let a man examine himself, and so let him eat of that bread, and drink of that cup.'
110. See Heinrich Heine, 'Die Heimkehr' ('The Homecoming'), 1823–4, *Buch der Lieder* (Leipzig, 1911, pp. 140–41).
111. The Royal Law was the foundation of Danish law until the new constitution of 1848.
112. Docetism is the heresy that Christ's body was not human but formed of celestial substance (from the Greek δοκεῖν, *dokein*, seem).
113. See n. 58.

1756 Michael Pedersen Kierkegaard, Søren's father, born in formal bondage of peasant stock in Sreding, West Jutland. Baptized 12 December.

1768 Michael Kierkegaard apprenticed to his uncle, a hosier, in Copenhagen. Ane Sørensdatter Lund, Søren's mother, born 18 June in south-east Jutland.

1777 The Sreding village priest formally releases Michael Kierkegaard from serfdom.

1788 Michael Kierkegaard receives royal patent 'to deal in East Indian and Chinese goods, as well as goods coming from our West Indian islands ... and to sell same at wholesale or retail to all and sundry'. This was the year that Arthur Schopenhauer was born.

1794 Michael Kierkegaard marries Kirstine Røyen, sister of a business partner.

1796 23 March, Kirstine Røyen Kierkegaard dies childless; Michael Kierkegaard inherits from his uncle and benefactor.

1797 Michael Kierkegaard retires from business in February. On 26 April, he marries Kirstine's maid, and his own distant cousin, Ane Sørensdatter Lund, at the family home on Købmagergade in Copenhagen. A daughter, Maren Kirstine, is born 7 September.

1799 25 October, a second daughter, Nicoline Christine, is born.

1801 7 September, a third, Petrea Severine, is born.

1805 A first son, Peter Christian, is born.

1807 23 March, a second son, Søren Michael, is born.

1808 The year in which Hans Lassen Martensen, Kierkegaard's tutor to be, rival and bitter opponent, was born.

1809 30 April, a third son, Niels Andrea, is born.

1813 5 May, a last child, Søren Aabye, is born at home (2 Nytorv), and baptized in the Church of the Holy Spirit 3 June. This was the year the State Bank was declared bankrupt, as a result of economic problems stemming from the bombardment of Copenhagen by the British fleet in 1807 and Denmark's continuing alliance with Napoleon. Other notable figures born that year were the composers Richard Wagner and Giuseppe Verdi.

1819 14 September, Kierkegaard's brother Søren Michael dies, aged twelve.

1821 Kierkegaard begins school at Copenhagen's Borger-dydskole.

1822 15 March, Maren Kirstine, Michael Kierkegaard's favourite daughter, dies, aged twenty-four.

1823 15 February, Regine Olsen, Kierkegaard's future fiancée, is born.

1828 20 April, Kierkegaard is confirmed in the Church of Our Lady by Pastor (later Bishop) J. P. Mynster.

1830 The year of the July Revolution, a three-day revolt in Paris that ends the Bourbon restoration, with its tightened control of the press and universities, and results in some degree of liberal reform. In Denmark, as elsewhere, one effect of the revolt was to consolidate the lobby for freedom of the press. Kierkegaard, who later takes part in the dispute over press freedom, graduates from the Borgerdydskole (with distinction in Greek, history, French and Danish composition) and on 30 October enters the University of Copenhagen. On 1 November he enlists in the King's Lifeguard, but four days later is discharged as unfit for service. His brother Peter Christian (known in academic circles as 'the disputing devil of the North'), who was in Paris at the time of the July Revolution, receives a doctorate from the University of Göttingen for a dissertation on telling lies.

1831 25 April, Kierkegaard takes the first part of the first-year university exam (with distinction in Latin, Greek, Hebrew, and history, and exceptional distinction in lower mathematics), and on 27 October the second part (with exceptional distinction in all subjects: theoretical and practical philosophy, physics and higher mathematics). This was the year that Hegel, whose influence on Danish philosophy provoked Kierkegaard's later onslaught on Hegelianism, died.

1832 Kierkegaard's 33-year-old sister Nicoline Christine (married to a clothier, Johan Christian Lund) dies after childbirth.

1832 His brother Niels Andreas emigrates to the USA to pursue a business career.

1833 21 September, Niels Andreas dies, twenty-four years old, in Paterson, New Jersey.

1834 31 July, his mother dies. 4 December, he makes his journalistic debut, under the imprint 'A', with a piece in *Flyveposten* (The Flying Post) entitled 'Also a Defence of Woman's Superior Capacity', in response to an article on the same theme. 29 December, his sister Petrea Severine (married to a banker, Heinrich Ferdinand Lund) dies after childbirth. Friedrich Schleiermacher, the Christian theologian and philosopher, also died this year, having visited and been fêted in Copenhagen only the year before.

1835 He spends a summer holiday at Gilleleje in northern Sjælland. Records his resolve 'to find a truth that is true for me, to find the idea for which I am willing to live and die.' 28 November, he reads a paper to the Student Union on 'Our Journal Literature' with reference to freedom of the press.

1836 He publishes (in *Flyveposten* and under the imprint 'B', but finally under his own name) three articles in an exchange on the topic of the paper delivered to the Student Union. Later in the year, his surviving brother Peter Christian marries and the couple make their home at 2 Nytorv.

1837 In May, he meets Regine Olsen (then fifteen years old) for the first time while visiting the Rørdam family in Frederiksberg. In September, he begins teaching Latin at the Borgerdysdskole and moves from Nytorv to his own apartment at 7 Løvstraede. In July, Peter Christian's young wife dies.

1838 13 March, Kierkegaard's mentor and mainstay, Poul Martin Møller, dies at forty-four. 9 August, his father dies and he inherits a sum amounting to near half a million dollars. In September he publishes his first book, *From the Papers of One Still Living*, attacking Hans Christian Andersen.

1839–40 He studies assiduously. In the winter he moves into an apartment at 11 Kultorvet, which he shares with another student. Ten months later he moves again, to 230A (now 38) Nørregade.

1840 He finally passes his examination for the theological degree (with distinction, though not at the top of the class), visits his ancestral home in Jutland, and, 10 September (having 'approached her for a month'), proposes to Regine Olsen, who is now eighteen years old to his twenty-seven. She accepts. In November, Kierkegaard enters the pastoral seminary for practical training in the ministry.

1841 12 January, he preaches a sermon in Holmen's Church. In July, his dissertation for the M.A. (later Ph.D.) degree. 'On the Concept of Irony', is accepted for public defence. 11 August, he breaks his engagement to Regine. 29 September, he successfully defends his dissertation. 11 October, the break with Regine is complete; 25 October, he leaves by ship for Berlin. He attends Schelling's lectures in Berlin, among others.

1842 Having written large parts of *Either/Or* in Berlin, he returns in March to Copenhagen to complete the work. Begins, but does not complete, or publish, 'De Omnibus Dubitandum Est'. Copenhagen this year saw the birth of Georg Brandes, a Danish intellectual who was to become an internationally famous literary critic and tried too late to interest Nietzsche in Kierkegaard's work.

1843 15 February, *Either/Or* published. May, he briefly visits Berlin. 8 May, two days before his departure, *Two Edifying Discourses* was published, followed 7 October by *Fear and Trembling* and *Repetition*, 13 October by *Three Edifying Discourses*, and 6 December by *Four Edifying Discourses*.

1844 24 February, Kierkegaard held, in the Church of the Trinity, and with 'distinction', the trial sermon required for entry into the Danish Church. *Two Edifying Discourses* and *Three Edifying Discourses* were published 5 March and 8 June respectively. Then in June *Philosophical Fragments*, *The Concept of Anxiety*, and *Prefaces*. In August followed *Four Edifying Discourses*. In October, he moves from 230A Nørregade back to the family house at 2 Nytorv. In the wider world, on which these works would later have some impact, this year saw the birth of Friedrich Nietzsche, whose father was born the same year as Kierkegaard.

1845 *Three Discourses on Imagined Occasions* and *Stages on Life's Way* are published in April on successive days. In May, he is away for two weeks on a brief visit to Berlin.

1846 In January, *The Corsair*, responding to a provocation signed by one of Kierkegaard's pseudonyms, attacks him in person. He briefly considers becoming a country pastor. *Concluding Unscientific Postscript* is published 27 February, followed on 30 March by *A Literary Review*. In May, he is absent once more from Copenhagen for a two-week trip to Berlin. In October, Meyer Goldschmidt, the editor of *The Corsair* and formerly a protégé of Kierkegaard, resigns and leaves Denmark.

1847 13 March, *Edifying Discourses in a Different Tenor* is published; 29 September, *Works of Love*. His publisher informs him that *Either/Or* is sold out. On 16 May, his rival and former tutor, Hans Lassen Martensen, is appointed Royal Chaplain. On 3 November, Regine marries her former teacher Friedrich Schlegel. In December, Kierkegaard sells the family home a 2 Nytorv. During the year he has twice visited his brother, now remarried and pastor at an out-of-town-parish at Pedersborg, near Sorø. Abroad, Marx and Engels are drafting the *Communist Manifesto*, which came out the following year.

1848 The year of the February Revolution in France with repercussions throughout Europe. These include the Dano-Prussian war over Schleswig-Holstein. His servant is drafted. Just previously, 20 January, King Christian VIII, with whom

Kierkegaard had at least two audiences, had died. On 28 January, he had signed a lease on an apartment at the corner of Rosenborggade and Tornebuskgade and in April moved in. On 26 April, *Christian Discourses* is published and 24 and 27 July the two-part article, 'The Crisis and a Crisis in an Actress's Life'. By November he has finished *The Point of View of My Work as an Author* but decides not to have it published in his lifetime. The year was also the gestation period for *The Sickness unto Death*, some conception for which is first mentioned in a journal entry from 28 December 1847.

1849 *The Lilies of the Field and the Birds of the Air* and *Two Minor Ethico-Religious Treatises* are published 14 and 19 May respectively. *The Sickness unto Death* is published 30 July under a new pseudonym, Anti-Climacus, and *Three Discourses at Communion on Fridays* 13 November.

1850 18 April, he moves to yet another apartment, at 43 Nørregade. *Practice in Christianity* is published under the Anti-Climacus pseudonym 27 September and *An Edifying Discourse* 20 December.

1851 In April, he moves outside the old city's walls to 108A Østerbro. On 18 May he gave a sermon at the Citadel Church, in August published *Two Discourses at Communion on Fridays* and *On My Work as an Author*, and 10 September *For Self-Examination*.

1852–3 In April, he moves back inside the city to a small two-room flat let out of a larger apartment at Klaedeboderne 5–6 (now 28 Skindergade and 5 Dyrkøb), just opposite the Church of Our Lady. *Judge for Yourself* is completed but not published until twenty-one years after his death. In his journals he reflects over his 'life's operation'.

1854 30 January, Bishop Mynster dies. In February, Kierkegaard writes an article attacking the established church, but does not publish it until December. Hans Martensen is named Bishop 15 April. Rather than provoking reaction, publication of the article causes some confusion.

1855 From January to the end of May, he attacks the church in various articles published in *Faedrelandet*. In this final year he publishes: 24 May, *This Must Be Said, So Let It Now Be Said*; 16 June, *Christ's Judgment on Official Christianity*; and 3 September, *The Unchangeableness of God*. In May he begins his own broadsheet, *The Instant*. It goes through nine issues before he falls ill. On 2 October, he collapses outside his home and is taken later, at his own request, to Frederiks Hospital. He dies there six weeks later, at 9 p.m., 11 November, probably of a staphylococcus infection of the lungs, though there was no autopsy. His funeral, at the prompting of his brother Peter Christian, but much to Martensen's distaste, was conducted at the Church of Our Lady, attracting people of all classes, while the burial itself was the occasion of a disturbance in which Kierkegaard's devoted but overwrought nephew deplored the fact that the Church (at his older uncle's instigation) had commandeered the proceedings.

1859 *The Point of View of my Authorship* is published by Peter Christian Kierkegaard.

1860 The death of Arthur Schopenhauer (b. 1788), whose works Kierkegaard first read with admiration and mixed appreciation in 1854.

1884 Hans Lassen Martensen dies.

1888 24 February, Peter Christian Kierkegaard dies, aged eighty-two, his mind unbalanced. Thirteen years earlier, he resigned his episcopate in Aalborg (1856–75) and resigned his civic rights, placing himself in legal custody.

1904 Regine Schlegel dies. Her husband, Fritz Schlegel, governor of the Danish West Indies from 1855 until 1860 (on his deathbed Kierkegaard jibed that Regine had always wanted to be a 'governess') and later an important city official in Copenhagen, had died in 1896.

A reasonably erudite reader looking for some scholarly enlightenment on *The Sickness unto Death* can be referred to two useful essay collections, an earlier one: *International Kierkegaard Commentary 19: The Sickness unto Death*, ed. Robert L. Perkins (Macon, GA: Mercer University Press, 1987), and the more recent *Kierkegaard Studies: Yearbook 1996*, ed. N. J. Cappelørn and Hermann Deuser (Berlin/New York: Walter de Gruyter, 1996). The discussions here should present few problems to those who have some overall grasp of the text itself.

For a generally accessible and comprehensive view of the cultural and political background to Kierkegaard's writings, see Bruce H. Kirmmse's *Kierkegaard in Golden Age Denmark* (Bloomington and Indianapolis: Indiana University Press, 1990).

A highly readable short introduction to Kierkegaard's life and works is Michael Watts' *Kierkegaard* (Oxford: Oneworld Publications, 2003).

For general surveys of Kierkegaard's works and essays relating them to more recent thought, see Gordon Marino and Alastiar Hannay (eds.), *The Cambridge Companion to Kierkegaard* (Cambridge: Cambridge University Press, 1998); Martin J. Matustik and Merold Westphal (eds.), *Kierkegaard in Post/Modernity* (Bloomington and Indianapolis: Indiana University Press, 1995); and Jonathan Rée and Jane Chamberlain (eds.), *Kierkegaard: A Critical Reader* (Oxford: Blackwell, 1998). The way Kierkegaard's thought relates to philosophy is the general topic of Alastair Hannay, *Kierkegaard and Philosophy: Selected Essays* (London and New York: Routledge, 2003).

The pioneering biography is Walter Lowrie's *Kierkegaard* (London, New York, Toronto: Oxford University Press, 1938). The later Josiah Thomson's *Kierkegaard* (New York: Alfred A. Knopf, 1973) presents a less saintly portrait, while Alastair Hannay's *Kierkegaard: A Biography* (Cambridge: Cambridge University Press, 2001) places Kierkegaard's thought and writings in the context of his life and contemporaries.

Those interested in the biographical backgrouncd should also read Bruce H. Kirmmse's excellent annotated collection, *Encounters with Kierkegaard: A Life as Seen by His Contemporaries*, tr. Bruce H. Kirmmse and Virginia R. Laursen (Princeton, NJ: Princeton University Press, 1996).

PENGUIN ⓟ CLASSICS

The Classics Publisher

'Penguin Classics, one of the world's greatest series' JOHN KEEGAN

'I have never been disappointed with the Penguin Classics. All I have read is a model of academic seriousness and provides the essential information to fully enjoy the master works that appear in its catalogue' MARIO VARGAS LLOSA

'Penguin and Classics are words that go together like horse and carriage or Mercedes and Benz. When I was a university teacher I always prescribed Penguin editions of classic novels for my courses: they have the best introductions, the most reliable notes, and the most carefully edited texts' DAVID LODGE

'Growing up in Bombay, expensive hardback books were beyond my means, but I could indulge my passion for reading at the roadside bookstalls that were well stocked with all the Penguin paperbacks . . . Sometimes I would choose a book just because I was attracted by the cover, but so reliable was the Penguin imprimatur that I was never once disappointed by the contents.

Such access certainly broadened the scope of my reading, and perhaps it's no coincidence that so many Merchant Ivory films have been adapted from great novels, or that those novels are published by Penguin' ISMAIL MERCHANT

'You can't write, read, or live fully in the present without knowing the literature of the past. Penguin Classics opens the door to a treasure house of pure pleasure, books that have never been bettered, which are read again and again with increased delight' JOHN MORTIMER

CLICK ON A CLASSIC
www.penguinclassics.com
The world's greatest literature at your fingertips

Constantly updated information on over 1600 titles, from
Icelandic sagas to ancient Indian epics, Russian drama to
Italian romance, American greats to African masterpieces

•

The latest news on recent additions to the list, updated
editions and specially commissioned translations

•

Original scholarly essays by leading writers: Elaine Showalter
on Zola, Laurie R. King on Arthur Conan Doyle, Frank
Kermode on Shakespeare, Lisa Appignanesi on Tolstoy

•

A wealth of background material, including biographies
of every classic author from Aristotle to Zamyatin, plot
synopses, readers' and teachers' guides, useful web links

•

Online desk and examination copy assistance for academics

•

Trivia quizzes, competitions, giveaways, news on
forthcoming screen adaptations

•

eBooks available to download

EDGAR ALLAN POE

The Fall of the House of Usher and Other Writings

*'And much of Madness and more of Sin
And Horror the Soul of the Plot'*

This selection of Poe's critical writings, short fiction and poetry demonstrates his intense interest in aesthetic issues, and the astonishing power and imagination with which he probed the darkest corners of the human mind. 'The Fall of the House of Usher' describes the final hours of a family tormented by tragedy and the legacy of the past. In 'The Tell Tale Heart', a murderer's insane delusions threaten to betray him, while stories such as 'The Pit and the Pendulum' and 'The Cask of Amontillado' explore extreme states of decadence, fear and hate. These works display Poe's startling ability to build suspense with almost nightmarish intensity.

David Galloway's introduction re-examines the myths surrounding Poe's life and reputation. This edition includes a new chronology and further reading.

'The most original genius that America has produced'
ALFRED, LORD TENNYSON

'Poe has entered our popular consciousness as no other American writer' *The New York Times Book Review*

Edited with an introduction by DAVID GALLOWAY

ROBERT LOUIS STEVENSON

The Strange Case of Dr Jekyll and Mr Hyde and Other Tales of Terror

*'He put the glass to his lips and drank at one gulp
... his face became suddenly black and the
features seemed to melt and alter'*

Published as a 'shilling shocker', Robert Louis Stevenson's dark psychological fantasy gave birth to the idea of the split personality. The story of respectable Dr Jekyll's strange association with 'damnable young man' Edward Hyde; the hunt through fog-bound London for a killer; and the final revelation of Hyde's true identity is a chilling exploration of humanity's basest capacity for evil. The other stories in this volume also testify to Stevenson's inventiveness within the Gothic tradition: 'Olalla', a tale of vampirism and tainted family blood, and 'The Body Snatcher', a gruesome fictionalization of the exploits of the notorious Burke and Hare.

This edition contains a critical introduction by Robert Mighall, which discusses class, criminality and the significance of the story's London setting. It also includes an essay on the scientific contexts of the novel and the development of the idea of the Jekyll-and-Hyde personality.

Edited with an introduction and notes by ROBERT MIGHALL

THOMAS DE QUINCEY
Confessions of an English Opium-Eater

'Thou hast the keys of Paradise, oh just, subtle, and mighty opium!'

Confessions is a remarkable account of the pleasures and pains of worshipping at the 'Church of Opium'. Thomas De Quincey consumed daily large quantities of laudanum (at the time a legal painkiller), and this autobiography of addiction hauntingly describes his surreal visions and hallucinatory nocturnal wanderings though London, along with the nightmares, despair and paranoia to which he became prey. The result is a work in which the effects of drugs and the nature of dreams, memory and imagination are seamlessly interwoven. *Confessions* forged a link between artistic self-expression and addiction, paving the way for later generations of literary drug-users from Baudelaire to Burroughs, and anticipating psychoanalysis with its insights into the subconscious.

This edition is based on the original serial version of 1821, and reproduces the two 'sequels', 'Suspiria De Profundis' (1845) and 'The English Mail-Coach' (1849). It also includes a critical introduction discussing the romantic figure of the addict and the tradition of confessional literature, and an appendix on opium in the nineteenth century.

Edited with an introduction by BARRY MILLIGAN

OSCAR WILDE

The Picture of Dorian Gray

*'The horror, whatever it was, had not yet entirely
spoiled that marvellous beauty'*

Enthralled by his own exquisite portrait, Dorian Gray
exchanges his soul for eternal youth and beauty. Influenced by
his friend Lord Henry Wotton, he is drawn into a corrupt
double life, indulging his desires in secret while remaining a
gentleman in the eyes of polite society. Only his portrait bears
the traces of his decadence. *The Picture of Dorian Gray* was a
succès de scandale. Early readers were shocked by its hints at
unspeakable sins, and the book was later used as evidence
against Wilde at his trial at the Old Bailey in 1895.

This definitive edition includes a selection of contemporary
reviews condemning the novel's immorality, and the introduction to the first Penguin Classics edition by Peter Ackroyd.

Edited with an introduction and notes by ROBERT MIGHALL

CHARLES DICKENS
Bleak House

*'Jarndyce and Jarndyce has passed into a joke.
That is the only good that has ever come of it'*

As the interminable case of Jarndyce and Jarndyce grinds its
way through the Court of Chancery, it draws together a dis-
parate group of people: Ada and Richard Clare, whose inheritance is gradually being devoured by legal costs; Esther
Summerson, a ward of court, whose parentage is a source of
deepening mystery; the menacing lawyer Tulkinghorn; the
determined sleuth Inspector Bucket; and even Jo, a destitute
little crossing-sweeper. A savage but often comic indictment of
a society that is rotten to the core, *Bleak House* is one of
Dickens's most ambitious novels, with a range that extends
from the drawing-rooms of the aristocracy to the poorest of
London slums.

This edition follows the first book edition of 1853. Terry
Eagleton's preface examines characterization and considers
Bleak House as an early work of detective fiction.

**'Perhaps his best novel ... when Dickens wrote *Bleak House* he
had grown up' G. K. CHESTERTON**

'One of the finest of all English satires' TERRY EAGLETON

Edited with an introduction and notes by NICOLA BRADBURY
With a new preface by TERRY EAGLETON

BRAM STOKER

Dracula

'Alone with the dead! I dare not go out, for I can hear the low howl of the wolf through the broken window'

When Jonathan Harker visits Transylvania to help Count Dracula purchase a London house, he makes horrifying discoveries about his client and his castle. Soon afterwards, disturbing incidents unfold in England: an unmanned ship is wrecked at Whitby; strange puncture marks appear on a young woman's neck; and a lunatic asylum inmate raves about the imminent arrival of his 'Master'. In the ensuing battle of wits between the sinister Count and a determined group of adversaries, Bram Stoker created a masterpiece of the horror genre, probing deeply into human identity, sanity and the dark corners of Victorian sexuality and desire.

For this completely updated edition, Maurice Hindle has revised his introduction, list of further reading and notes, and added two new appendices: Stoker's essay on censorship and his interview with Winston Churchill, both published in 1908. Christopher Frayling's preface discusses Stoker's significance and the influences that contributed to his creation of the *Dracula* myth.

Edited with an introduction and notes by MAURICE HINDLE
With a preface by CHRISTOPHER FRAYLING

MARY SHELLEY

Frankenstein

*'Now that I had finished, the beauty of the
dream vanished, and breathless horror and
disgust filled my heart ...'*

Obsessed with creating life itself, Victor Frankenstein plunders
graveyards for the material to fashion a new being, which he
shocks into life with electricity. But his botched creature, rejected by Frankenstein and denied human companionship, sets
out to destroy his maker and all that he holds dear. Mary
Shelley's chilling Gothic tale was conceived when she was only
eighteen, living with her lover Percy Shelley near Byron's villa
on Lake Geneva. It would become the world's most famous
work of horror fiction, and remains a devastating exploration of
the limits of human creativity.

Based on the third edition of 1831, this volume contains all the
revisions Mary Shelley made to her story, as well as her 1831
introduction and Percy Bysshe Shelley's preface to the first
edition. This revised edition includes as appendices a select col-
lation of the texts of 1818 and 1831 together with 'A Fragment'
by Lord Byron and Dr John Polidori's 'The Vampyre: A Tale'.

Revised edition
Edited with an introduction and notes by MAURICE HINDLE